"In Sicily the past is not dead, but rather accompanies one from cradle to grave, in festivals and games, in spectacles and in church in rites and in traditions; everywhere it lives and speaks..."

Giuseppe Pitre
student of Sicilian folklore

SICILIA
Festa de Pasqua

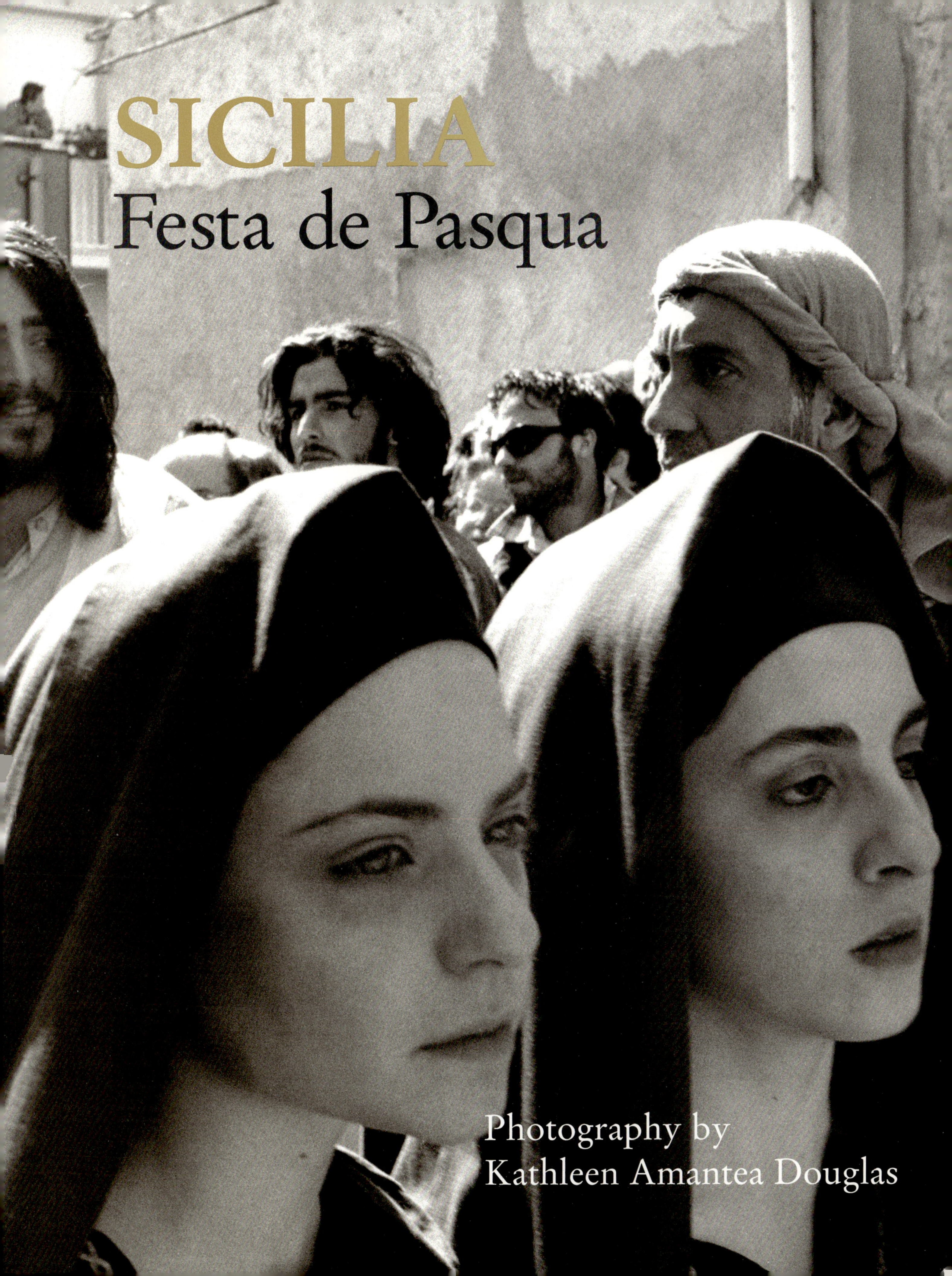

Photography by
Kathleen Amantea Douglas

In Appreciation

This book is dedicated to the people who are in it. To the people of Sicily whose enthusiastic kindness, deep passion for tradition and joy for life have moved me beyond expression.

Many people have helped me in the process of this book. I wish to thank Arthur Rainville whose editing, council and support have been invaluable to me. I wish to thank Costa Manos and Alex Majoli for their instruction and suggestion. Special thanks to my treasured Italian friends particularly Marco Garofalo who watched out for me like a son and my dear friend Carlo Bellavia who opened a window into the Sicilian heart.

Finally, I wish to express my profound admiration for my grand-parents Maria Rosa Lacona and Louigi Vittorio Amantea whose passion, courage and rock solid faith were the source of all that came after and the conduit for all that came before.

Photographs Edited by Arthur Levi Raineville

Known as an artist and innovator Mr.Rainville's personal work is exhibited in galleries from New York to Montreal and has been in featured display on three continents. A student of the Burano School in Italy Arthur is a well known presenter and offers enrichment programs to professional photographic organizations throughout the country. In addition to twelve years as Portrait Dept. Chair at the New England School of Photography, he teaches Concept Portraiture as a part of the TNT Tour nationwide. He also presents to non-photographic groups on journeys from his forthcoming book "Living Moments."

Introduction by Peter Southwick

Peter Southwick is a Director of Photojournalism and a Professor of Journalism at Boston University. Prior to coming to BU he was Photo Editor for the Boston Globe Magazine and worked as a photojournalist for Associated Press for fifteen years.

In God's Grace by Carlo Bellavia

Carlo Bellavia is a respected fine art photographer and a principal of a prominent family business where he works and lives in Palermo, Sicily.

Photograph of Kathleen Douglas: Arthur L. Raineville

ISBN# 0-9713154-7-7

SWC Editions
News and Book Publishers
LOS ANGELES

3940 Laurel Canyon Boulevard #698
Studio City, CA 91604
323.654.9339
www.stevenwaynecompany.com

Printed in Los Angeles by
FineArts Printing Services (866) 480-0550

Introduction

The duty of the photojournalist is to connect the life of the subjects she has chosen to those of her readers, people who may live thousands of miles away, separated by cultural as well as physical space. In order to make that connection, she must share the experiences of those isolated by her lens, while balancing on the thin divide between observation and participation. She must be aware of the passions of the moment, but avoid being swept so far into them that she no longer sees with the vision of the outsider. It is a demanding, delicate role that can be fulfilled only through determination and skill.

Kathleen Douglas strives for an even loftier goal, that of visual history. In her series of photographs of the Easter Processions of Sicily, she inhabits the marvelous landscape of rituals that claim roots dating back countless generations. The traditions themselves are a rich visual feast, but it is their enduring humanity that makes them survive through eons of challenge and change. It is the human connection that makes them compelling to an observer who may know nothing of their origins or significance. One doesn't need ancestry from this region to be moved by their solemnity, gaiety, and grace. Ms. Douglas's images succeed in connecting other members of the global family to this provincial celebration.

The photographs in this volume are visually arresting, commanding the attention of the viewer. They should not be looked at quickly, but instead they ask to be savored, to be viewed at sufficient length to appreciate all they have to offer. The images possess a strong sense of place, to be sure. But beyond that, they convey the nature of the people who inhabit them: passionate, devoted, intriguing, and vibrant. Their subjects are not relics of some ancient time, but contemporaries who feel the ties to generations past. And in these photos are surprises: a sidelong glance, a startling juxtaposition of elements, a stark contrast of shadow and light. Somber black and white tones mix with joyous splashes of color; razor sharp focus stands in relief against whirling motion. These images reflect both the choreography of an ancient ritual and the chaos of a modern celebration, and they allow the viewer to dance in the procession.

Kathleen Douglas writes of the Easter Processions that "participants and spectators are transported to a place beyond themselves..." She could as well be describing the effect of her own photographic essay, inviting viewers to experience what she has seen and expand their sense of community to a wider world.
Peter Southwick

December 2002

In God's Grace

Douglas' images embrace the deep passion the Sicilians hold for the religious tradition of their Easter processions. For the Sicilians the long wait of yet another year culminates in the longed for and heartfelt participation in the Passion of Christ during Holy Week.

With theatrical zeal and emotion, the people relive the series of events that led to Christ's crucifixion. The island, from the smallest village to the largest city, is transported back two thousand years in time as the Sicilians, both entire families of the Christian communities and individual believers crowd into every square to personally relive the pain, fatigue and desperation suffered by Christ in the days of his Passion.

Attending the Easter processions means being involved with the feelings, and experiencing the highly sentimentally charged atmosphere, which envelopes both the protagonists and spectators that flock to take part in the event.

Whether or not you are a believer makes no difference. It is an explosion of raw emotion: weeping, embracing, atonement and regeneration—all amid a myriad of colors. Douglas' compositions reveal a story of compassion, madness, silent consternation and the illusory--that sensation of being held in God's Grace.

It is with fortune and honor that participants share in this extraordinary religious event that vigorously refuses change and remains unaltered within the constant evolution of modern society.

Carlo Bellavia
Palermo

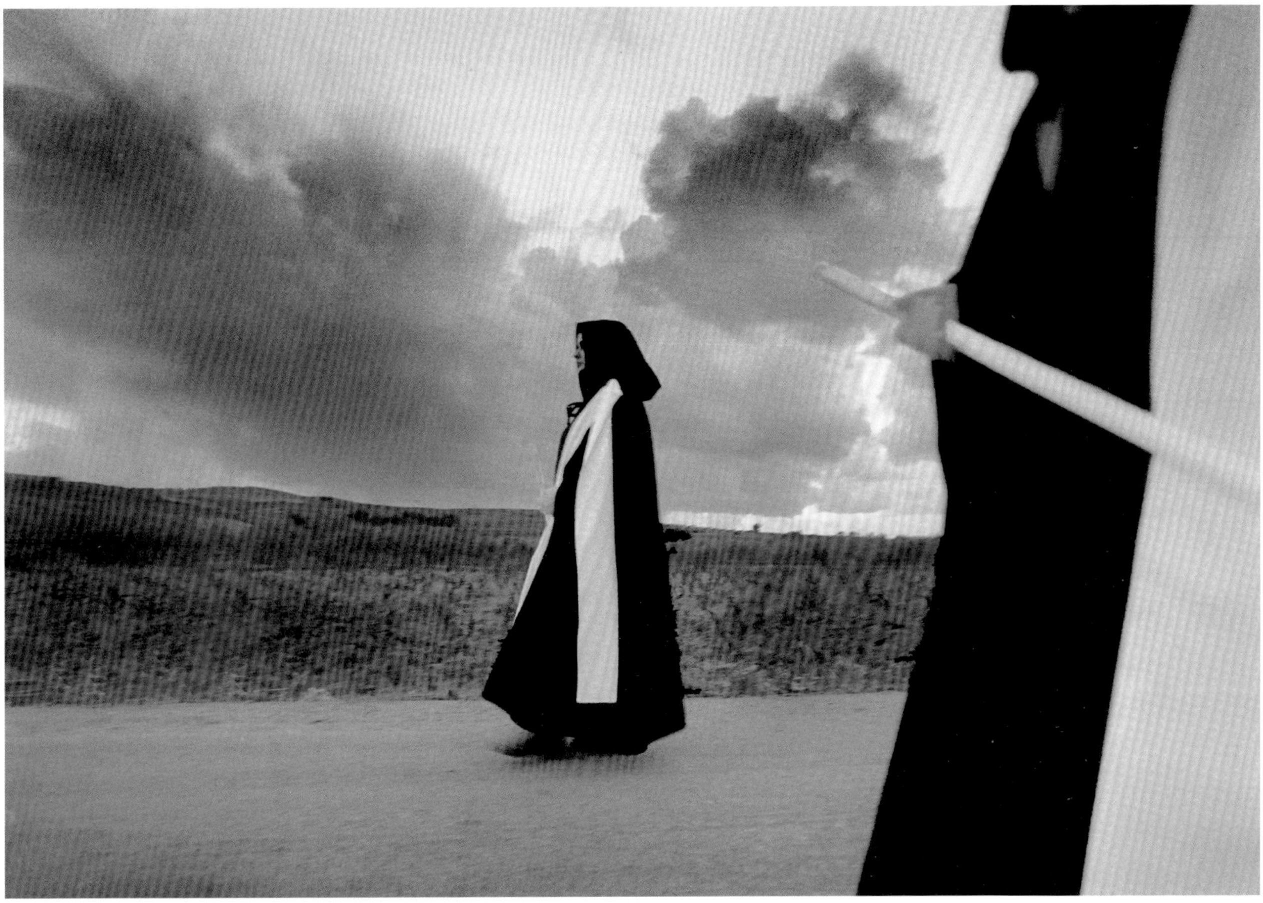

In Grace
Busteo Palizzolo

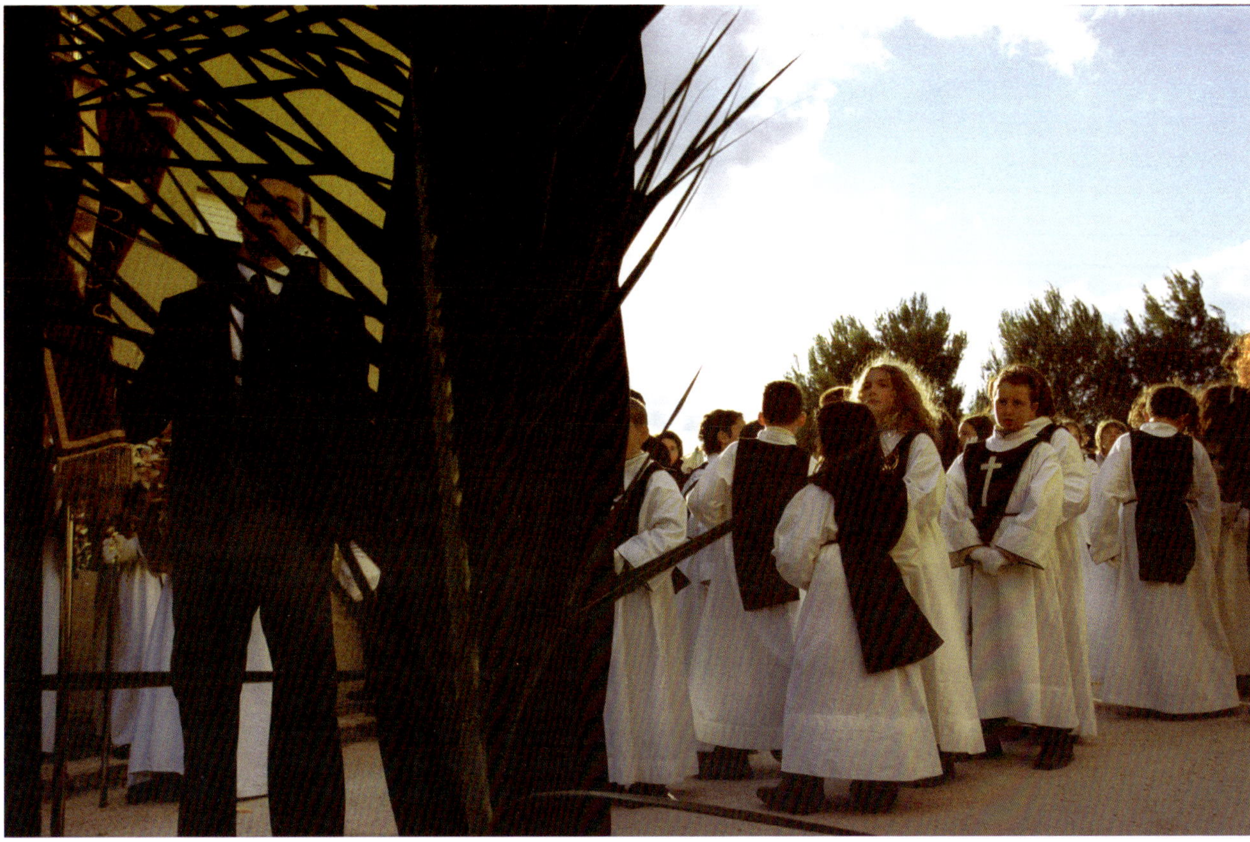

Palm Sunday
Busteo Palizzolo

Midweek in the days before Holy Saturday the Madonna moves through the streets searching for her son that has been arrested. The heavy statue of the Madonna in a Gilded Box is carried on the shoulders of pentinents with expressions of excruciating grimness. She sways back and forth, in and out, in slow deliberate rocking motion. Behind a brass band drones a solemn ad repitious dirge, "A Tear on My Mother's Grave". She is surrounded by candles and the wax drips on the bearers who wear it like a symbol of honor.

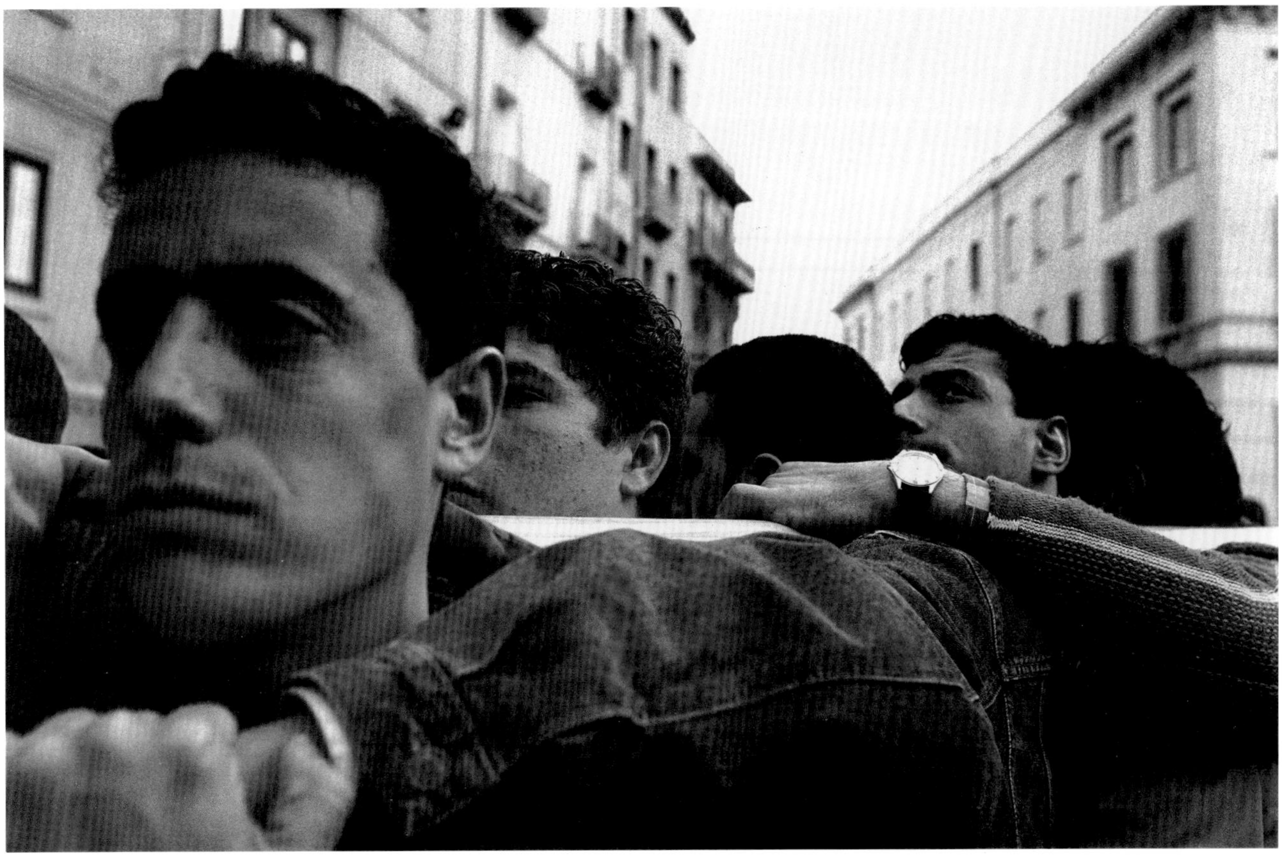

Young Bearers
Trapani

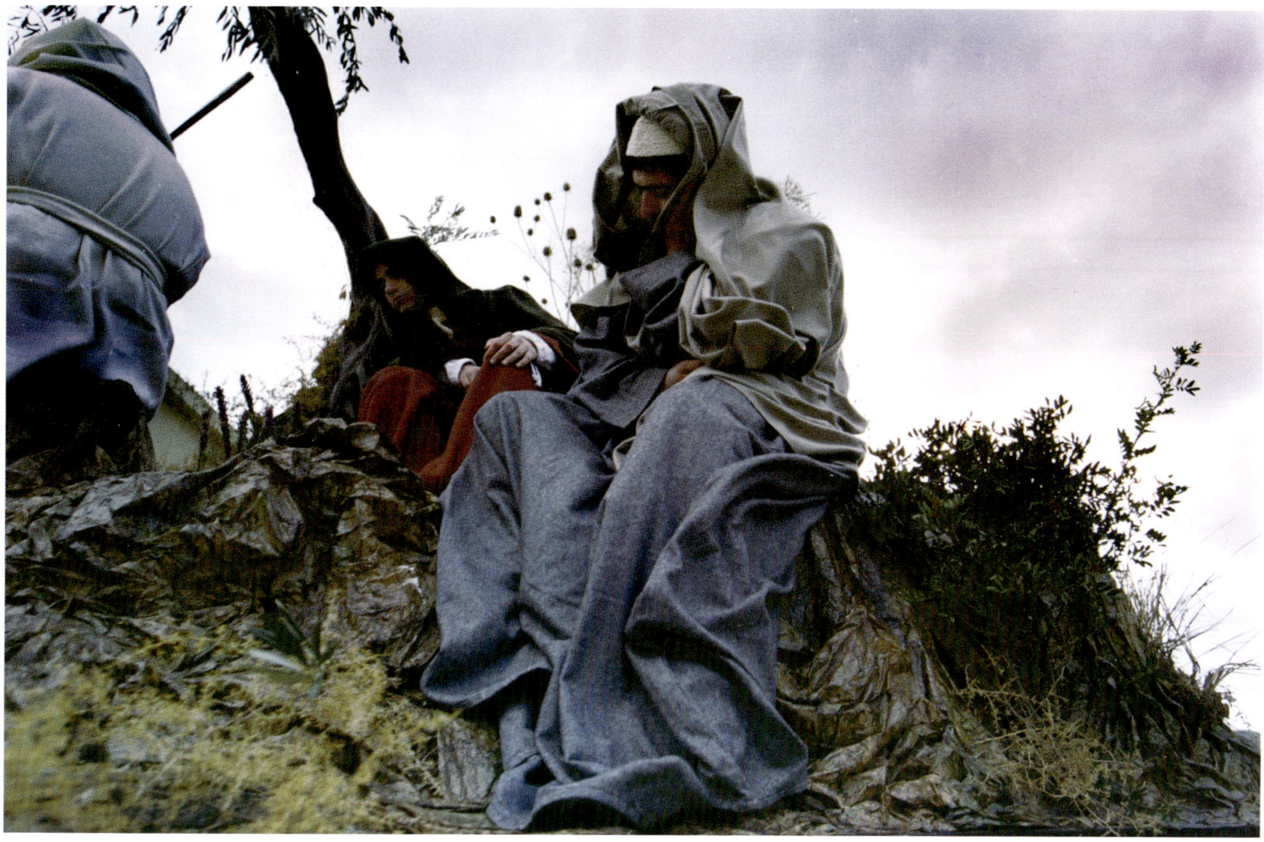

Mourners
Busteo Palizzolo

A reenactment of the life of Christ beginning with his teachings to the crowds to his agonizing crucifiction on Calvary are acted out in haunting realism. The sounds of Mary's agonizing screams draw cries as a soldier jerks the rope tied to a bloody Christ and he falls for the second time.

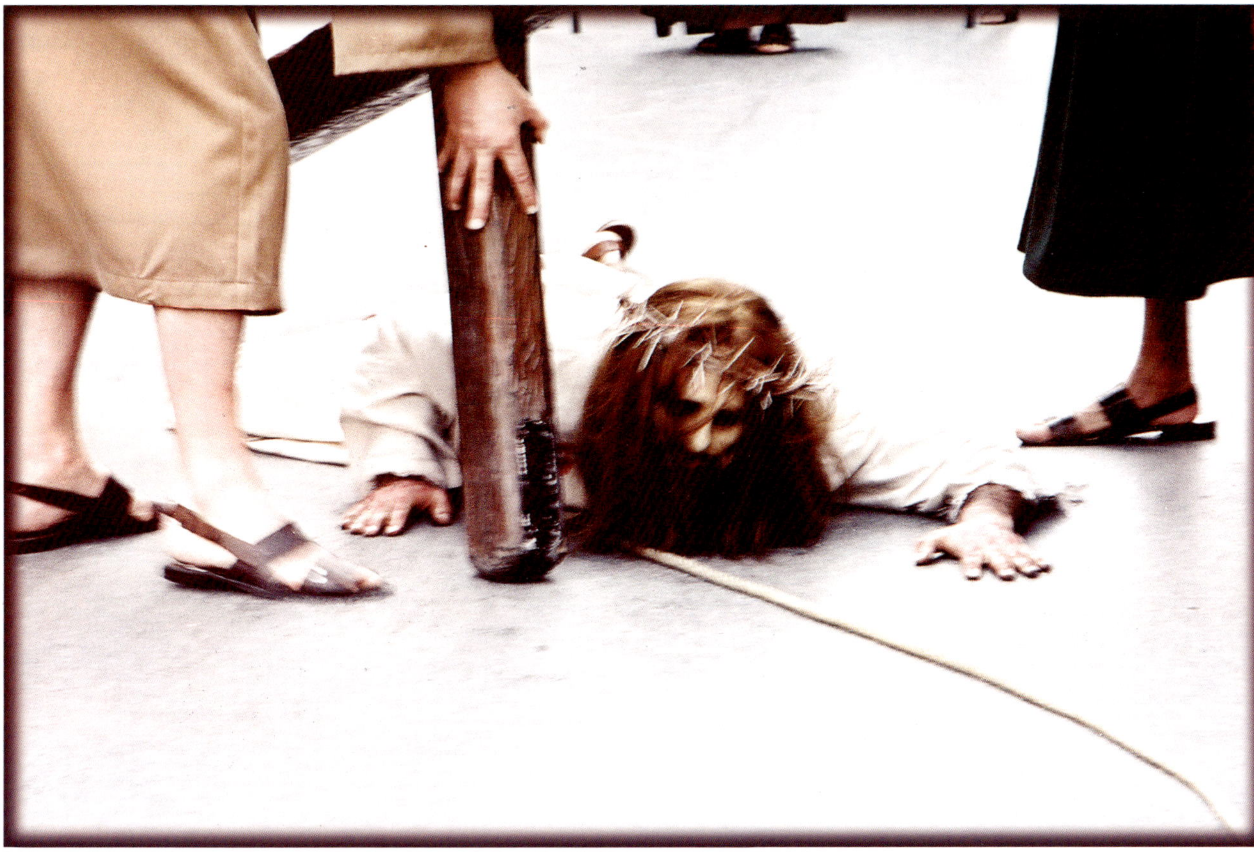

Christ Falls
Marsala

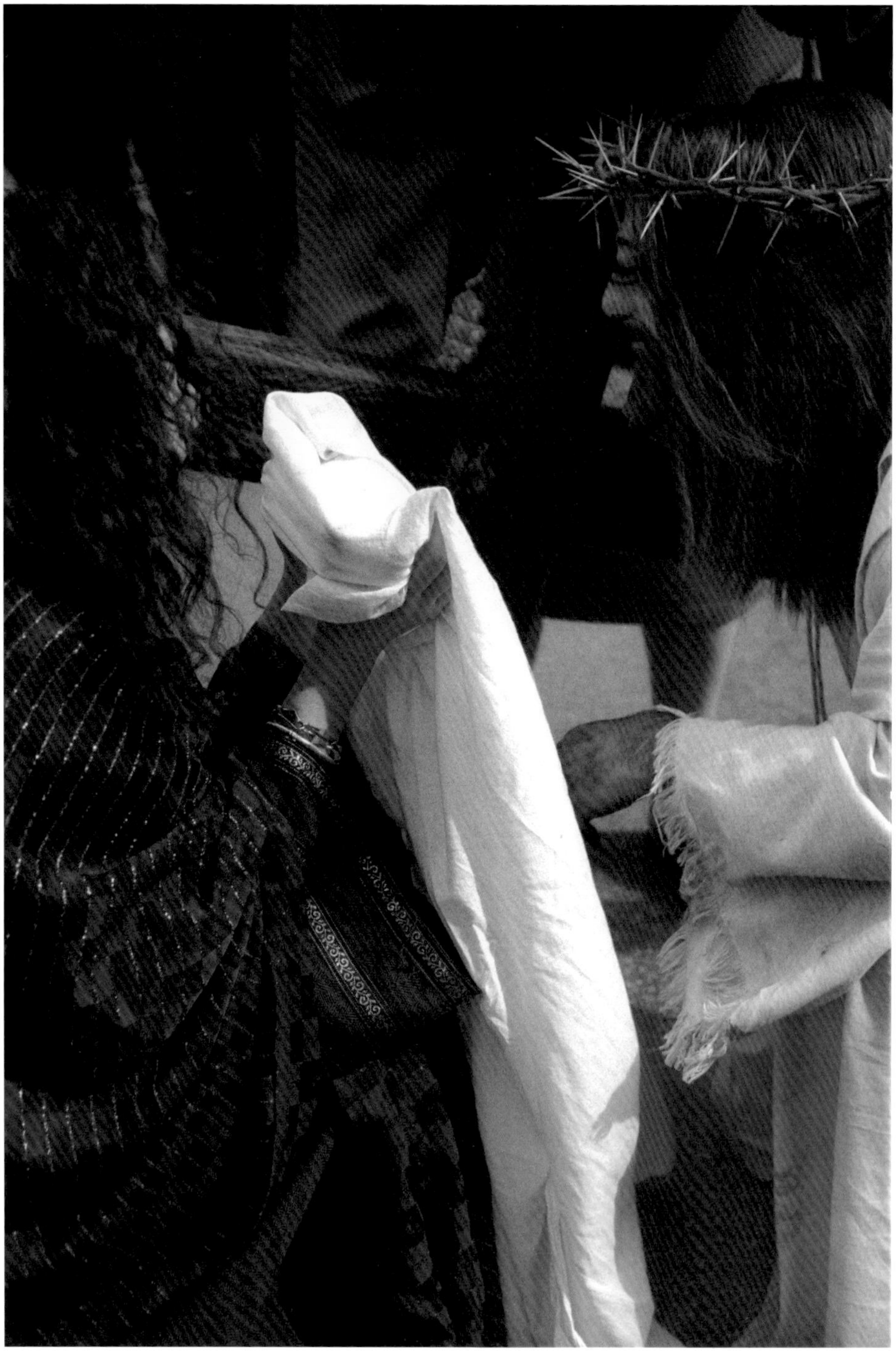

Veronica
Marsala

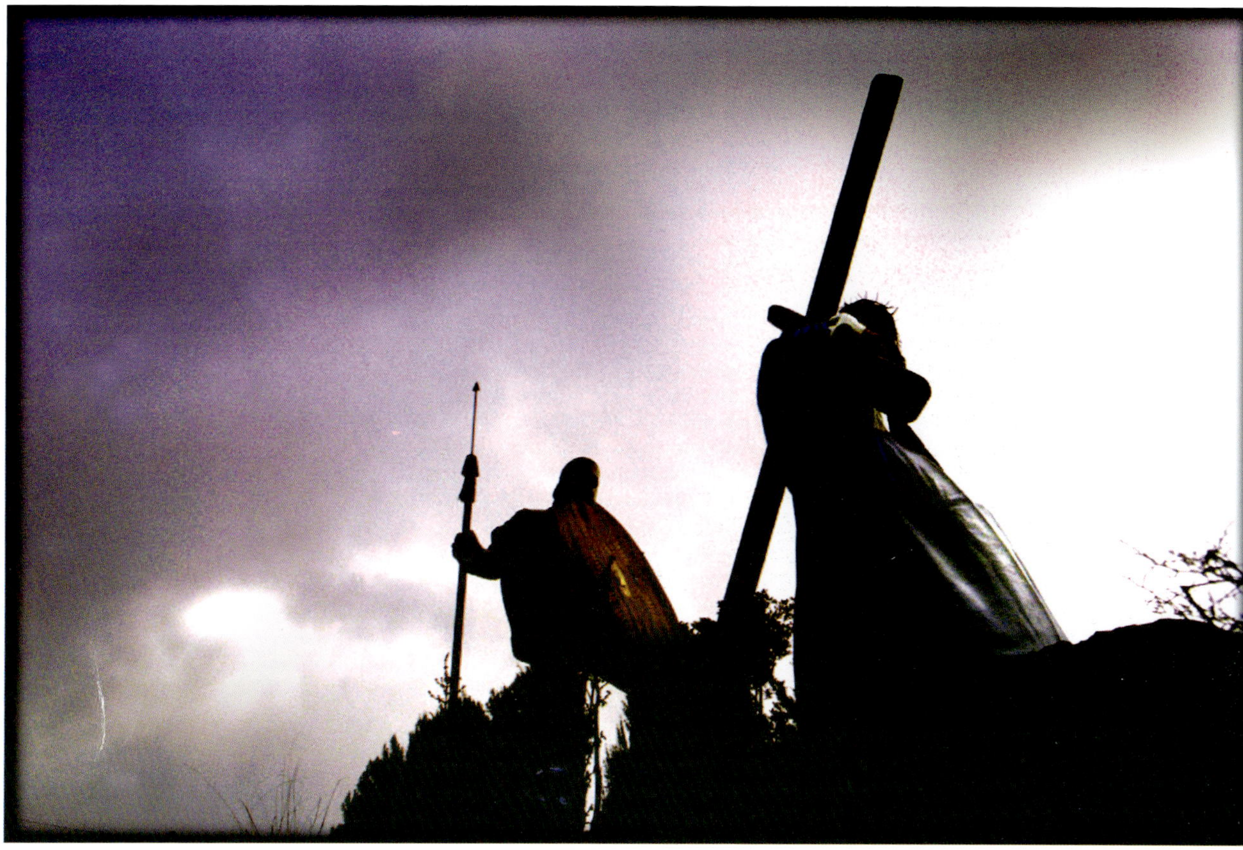

Towards Calvary
Busteo Palizzolo

A follower of Christ beseeches the crowd.

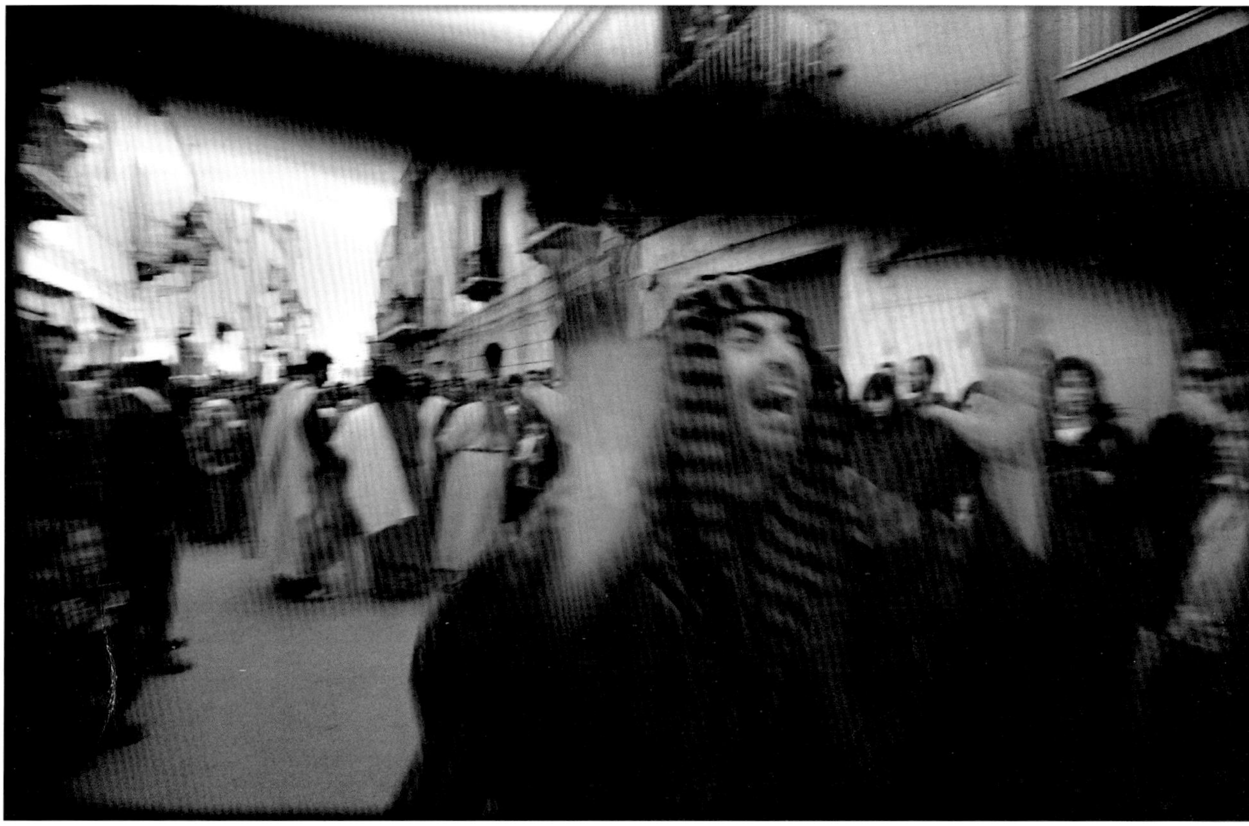

The Apostle
Marsala

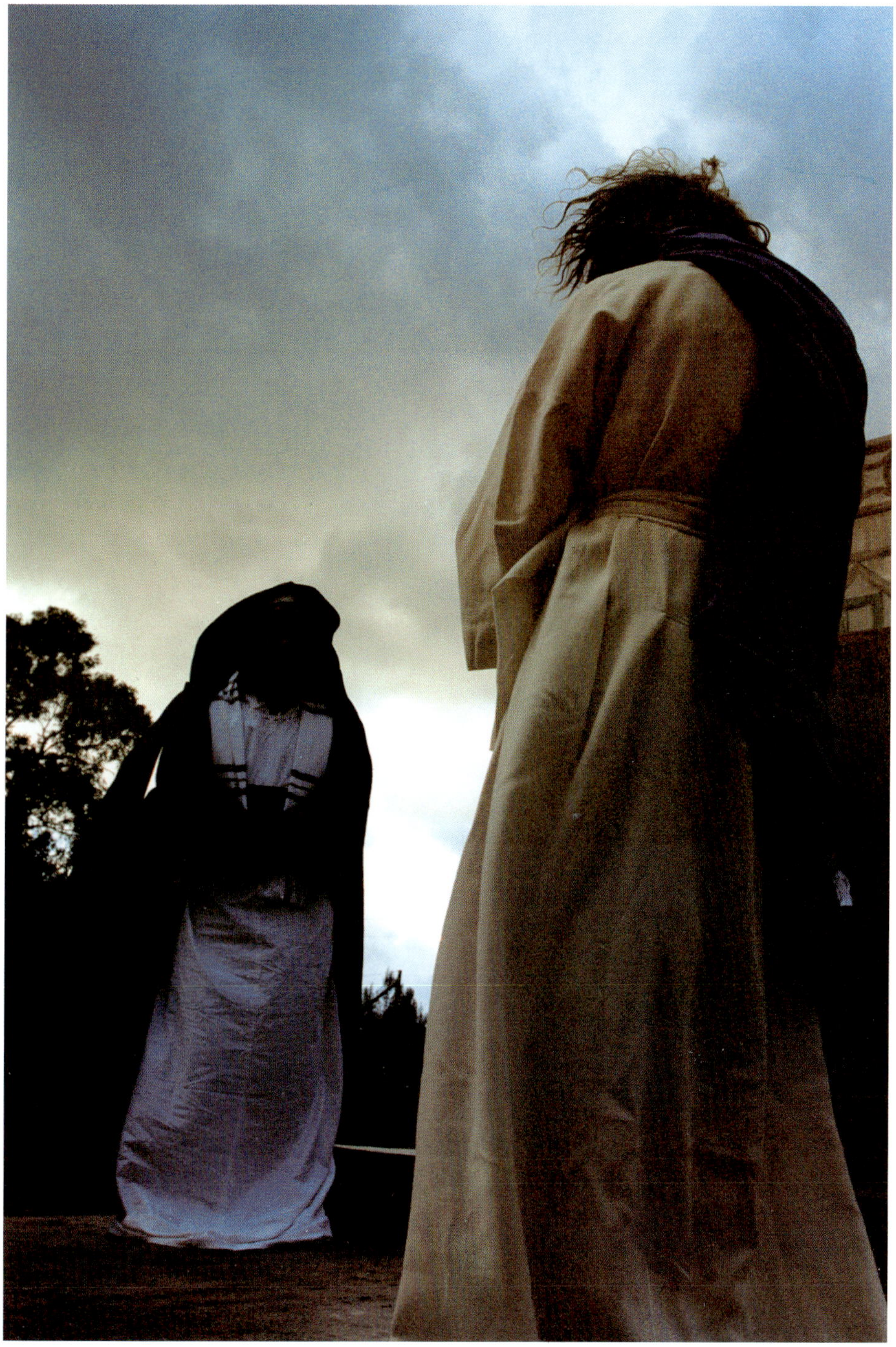

Judgement
Busteo Palizzolo

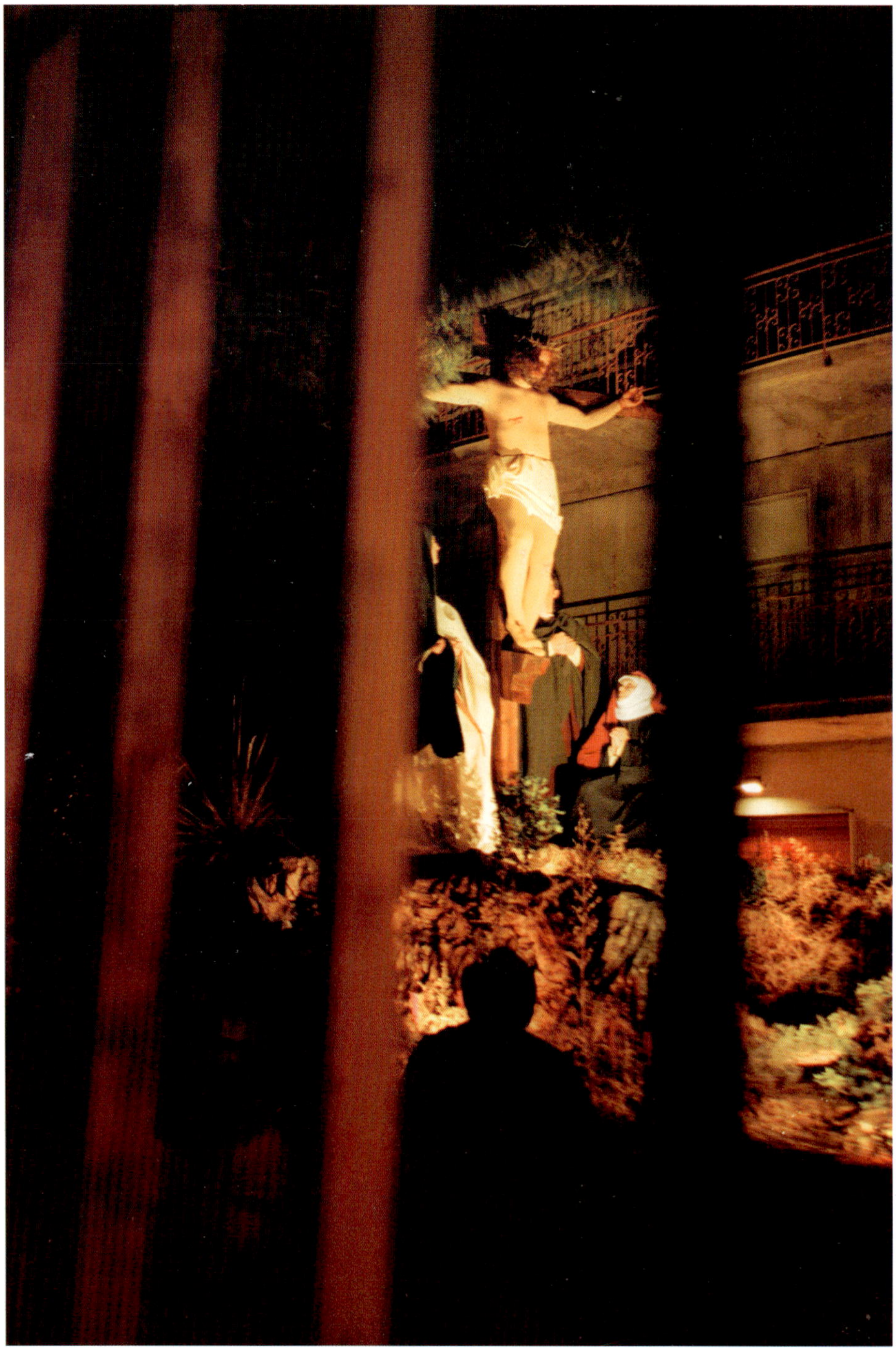

Gesù Muore in Croce
Busteo Palizollo

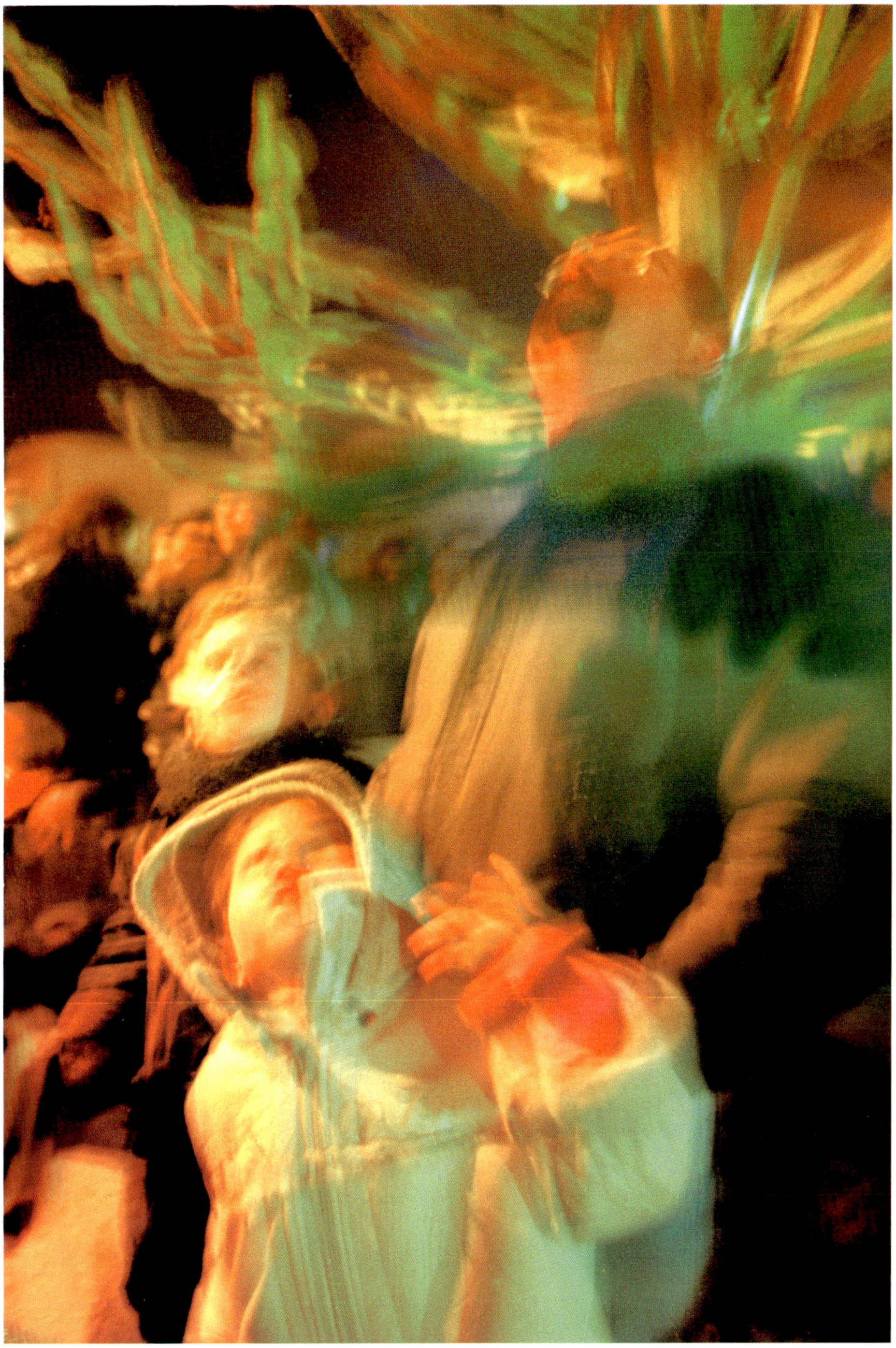

Behold
Busteo Palizollo

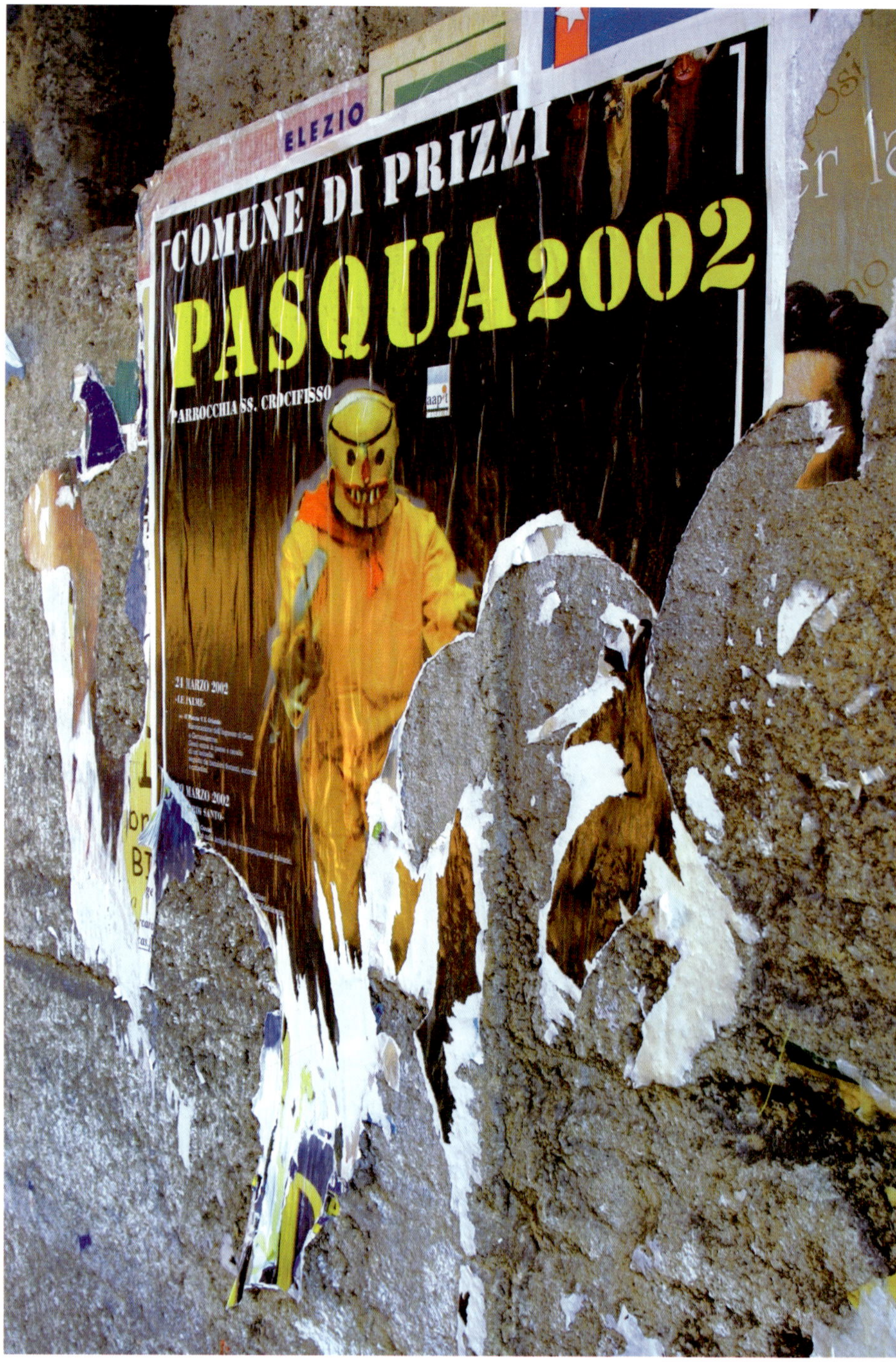

Pasqua 2002
Prizzi

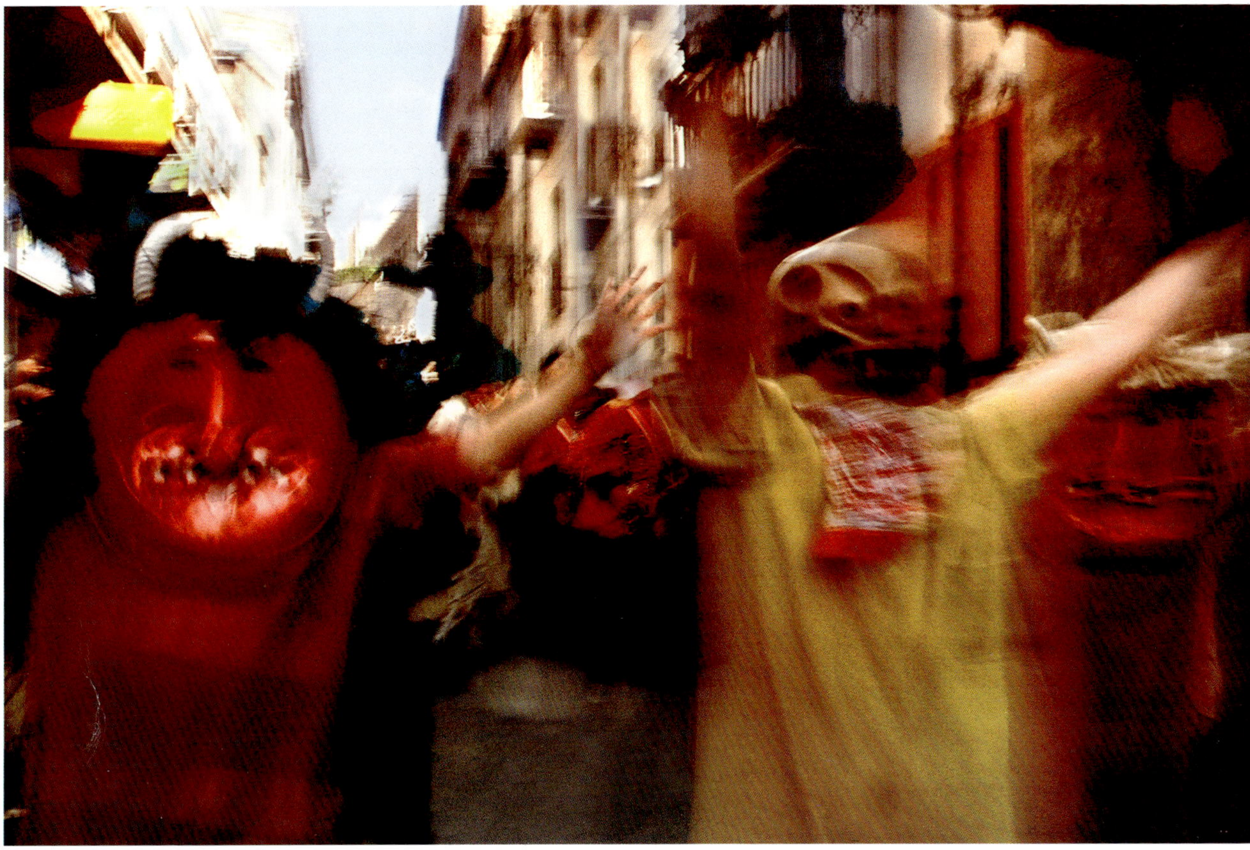

I Diavoli e La Morte
Prizzi

In pagan and erotic rhythms the devils dance as the forces of evil surround the Madonna cloaked in mourning.

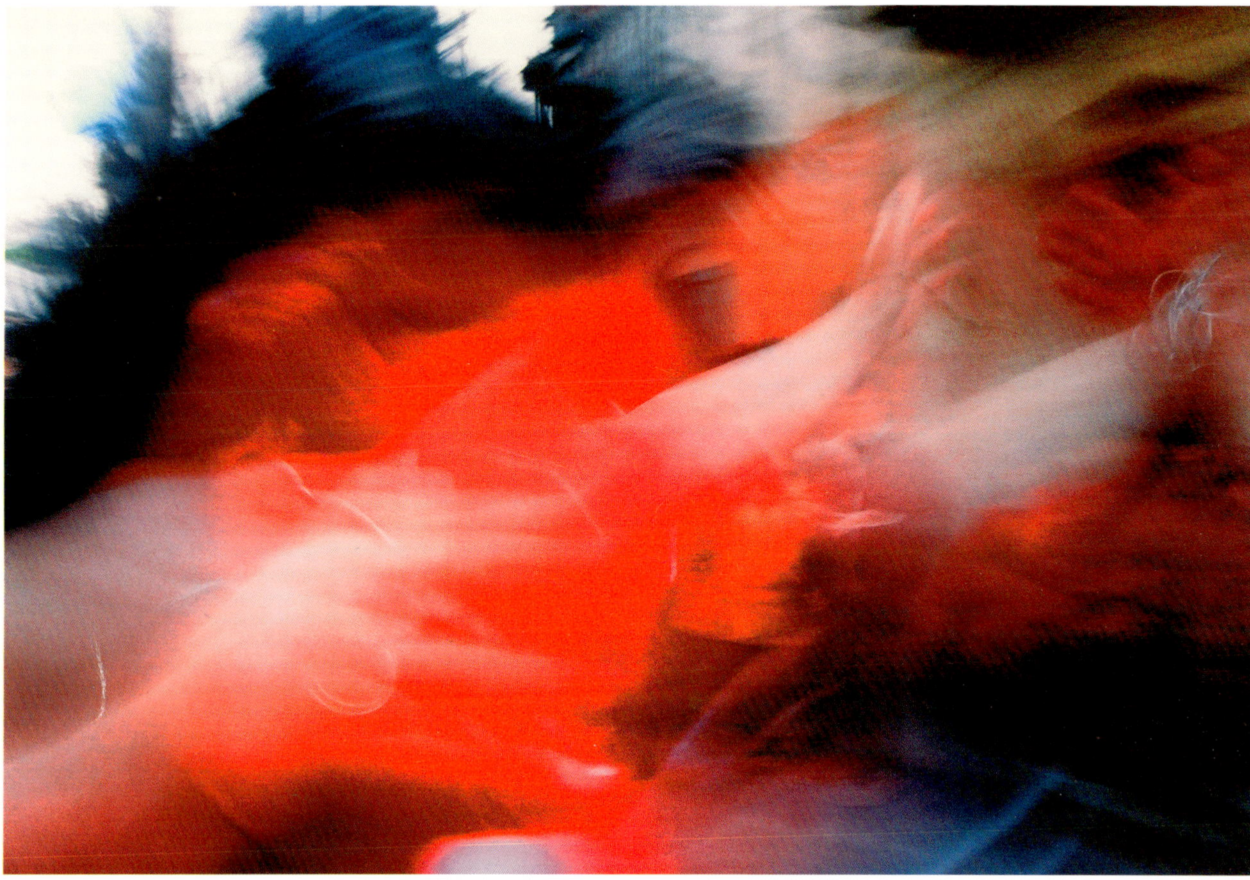

Ballo dei Diavoli
Prizzi

In a classic battle of good verses evil masked figures of Devils and Death dance in pagan rhythms besieging the Madonna until, together with the archangels, she triumphs. Her black cloak of mourning is discarded and she is rejoined with her son.

Liberated by his Mother and the archangels Christ moves through the streets of Prizzi

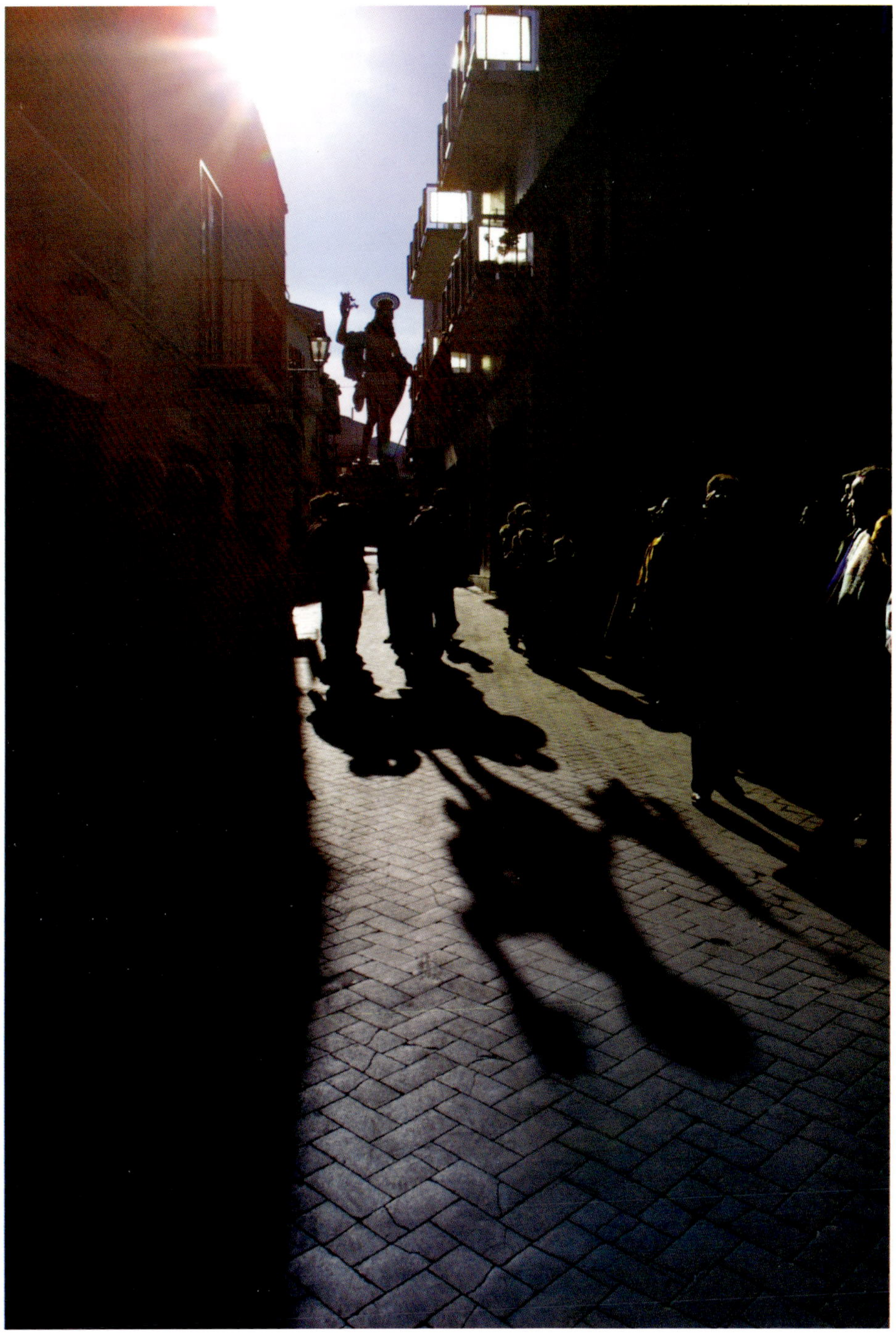

Liberated Christ
Prizzi

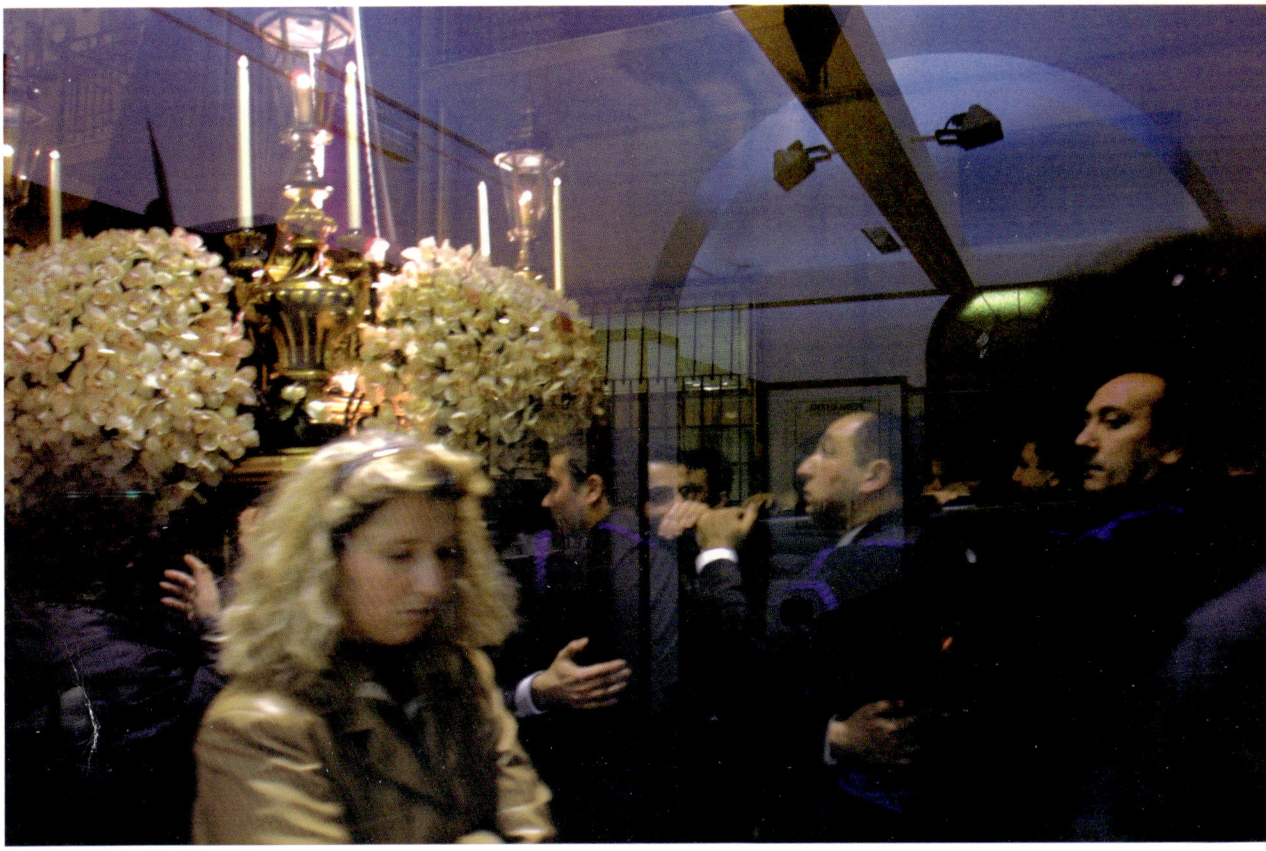

Reflections
Palermo

Shrouded woman carrying lit tapers walk in procession following the Madonna through the mountaintop city of Enna. Located in the Center of Sicily, Enna is also a mythical center. It was here at the Temple of Demeter where she celebrated the return of her abducted daughter Persephone from the underworld. Easter rites focus on the return of sacred children from the darkness.

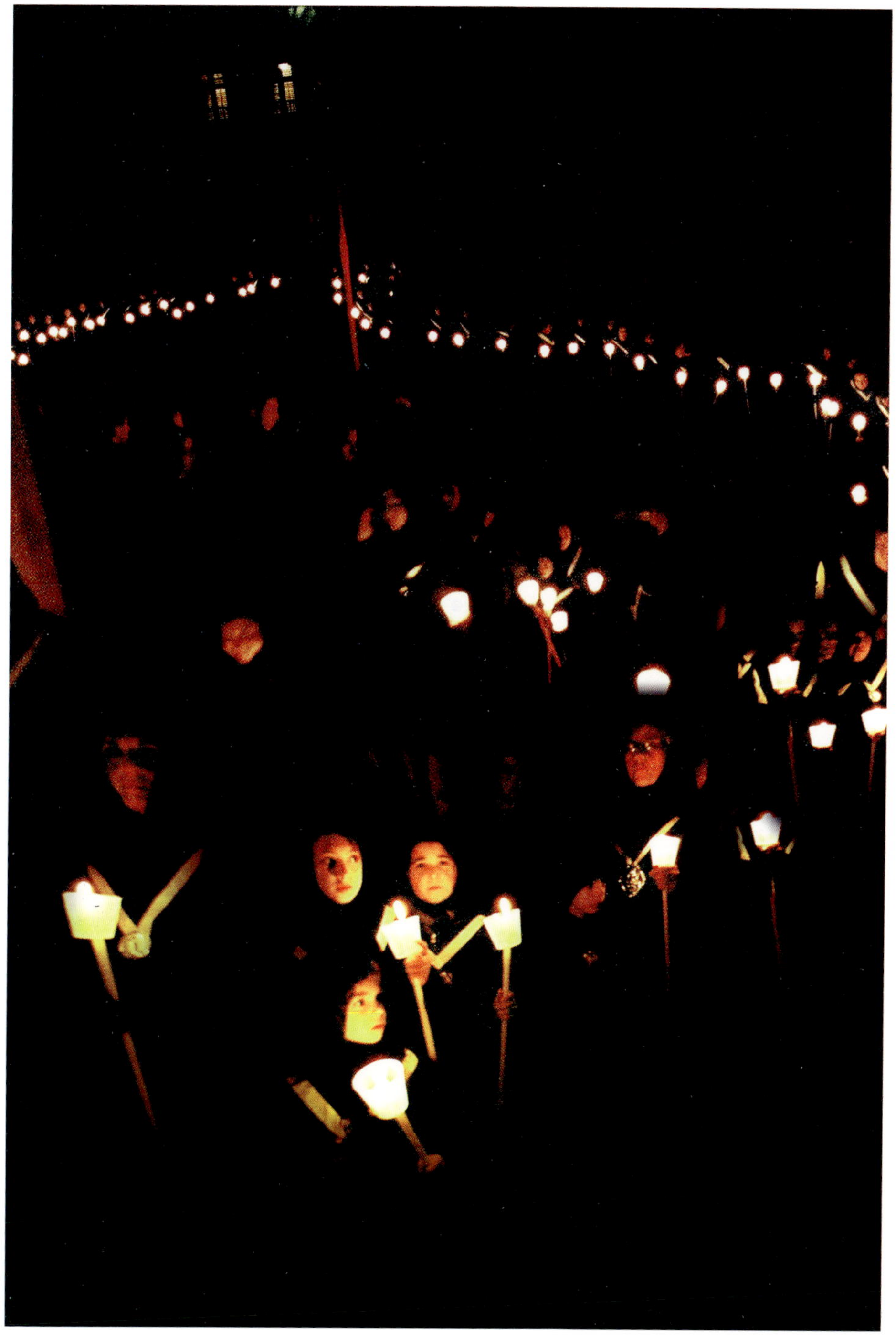

Procession
Enna

Influenced by a Spanish medieval past robed and hooded executioners move in an eeire night procession carrying lighted tapers.

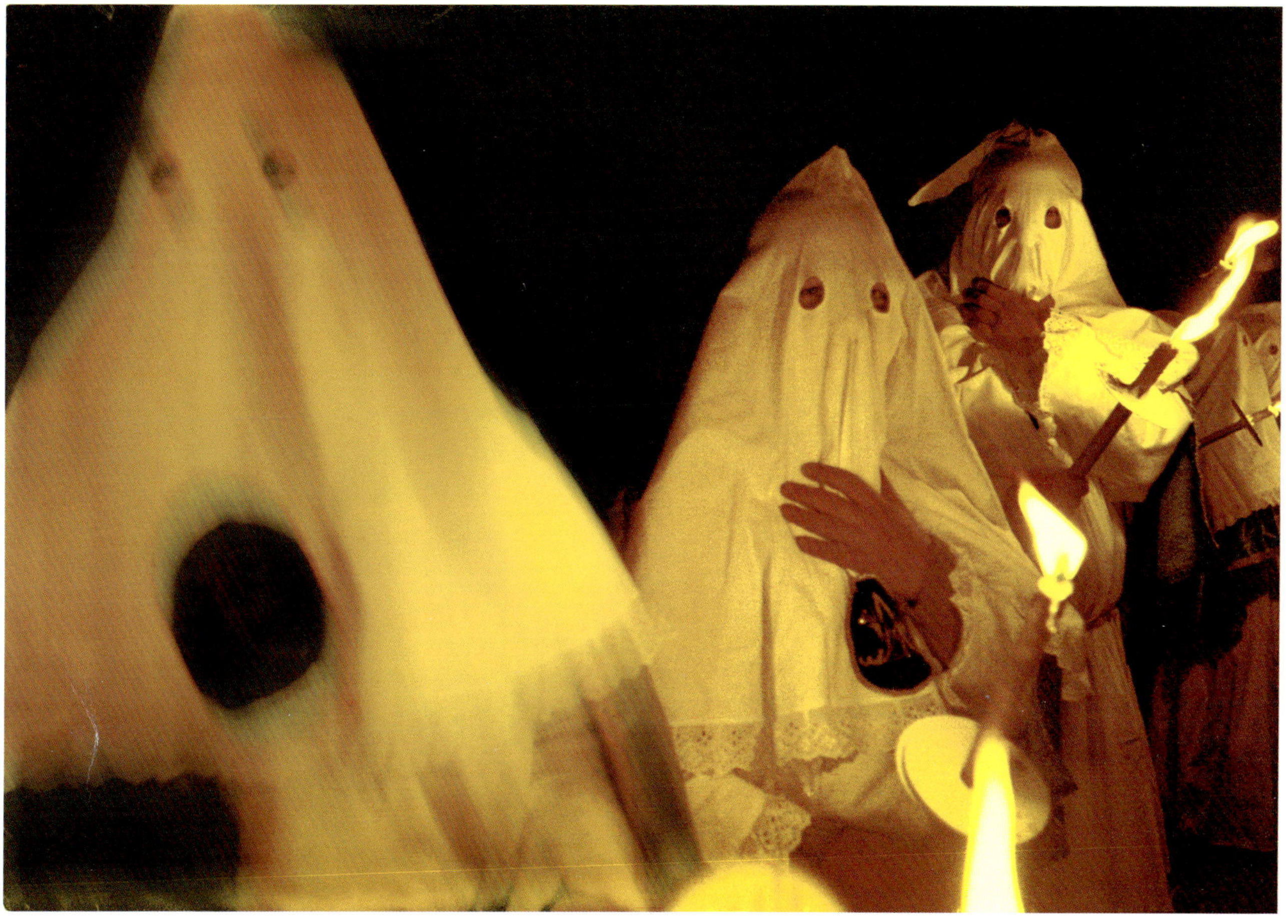

Executioners
Enna

The solemn cadence of the bands is an integral part of every procession. The monotonous and solemn dirge reverberates through the narrow cobbled streets.

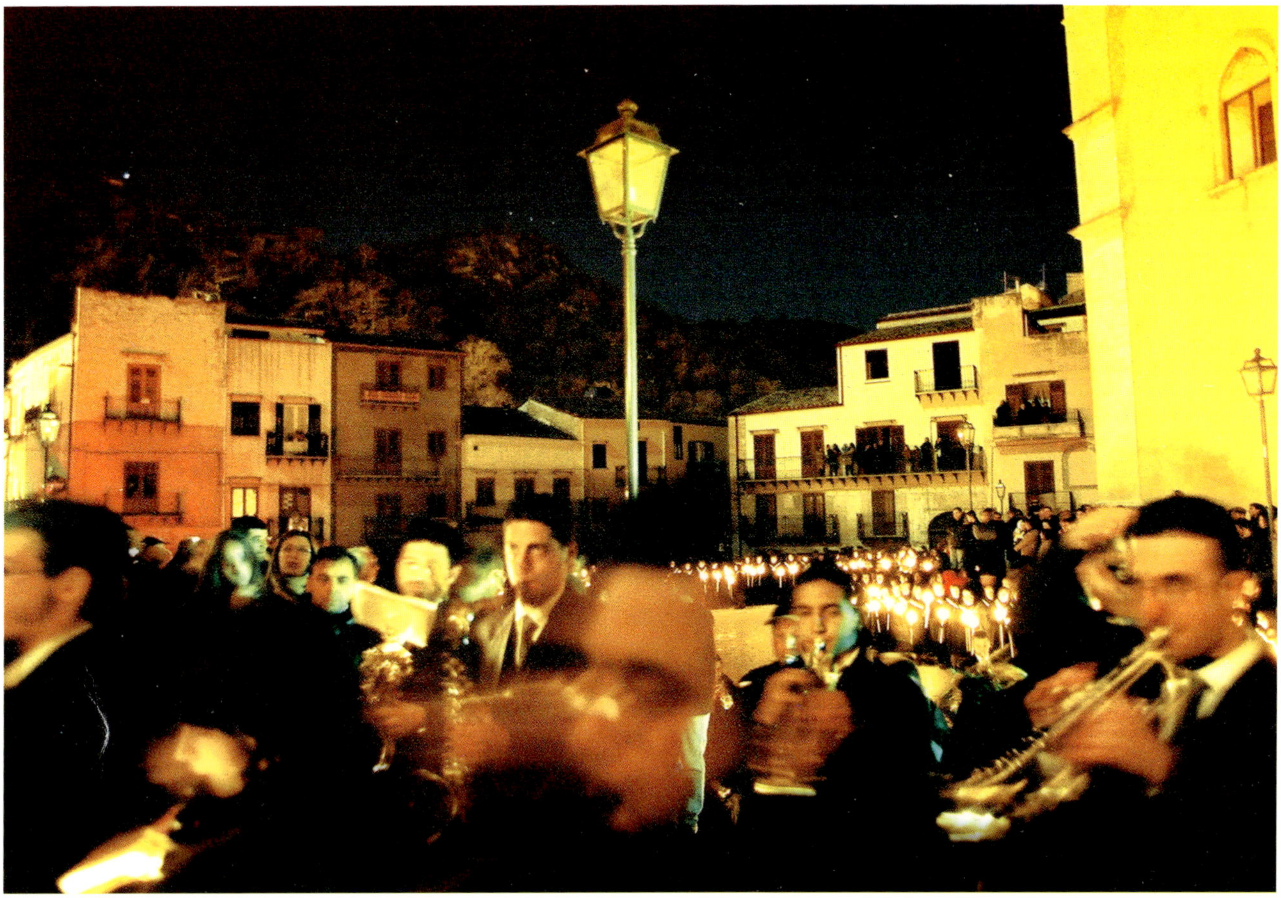

The Band at Enna
Enna

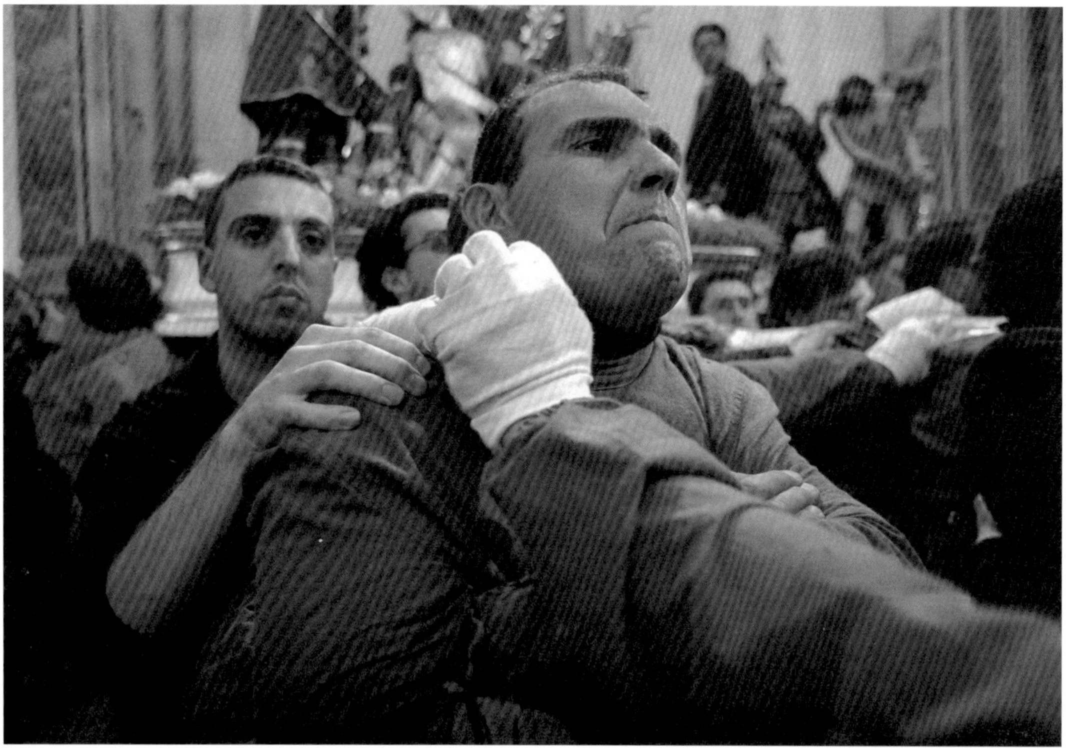

La Chiesa della Corrigio
Trapani

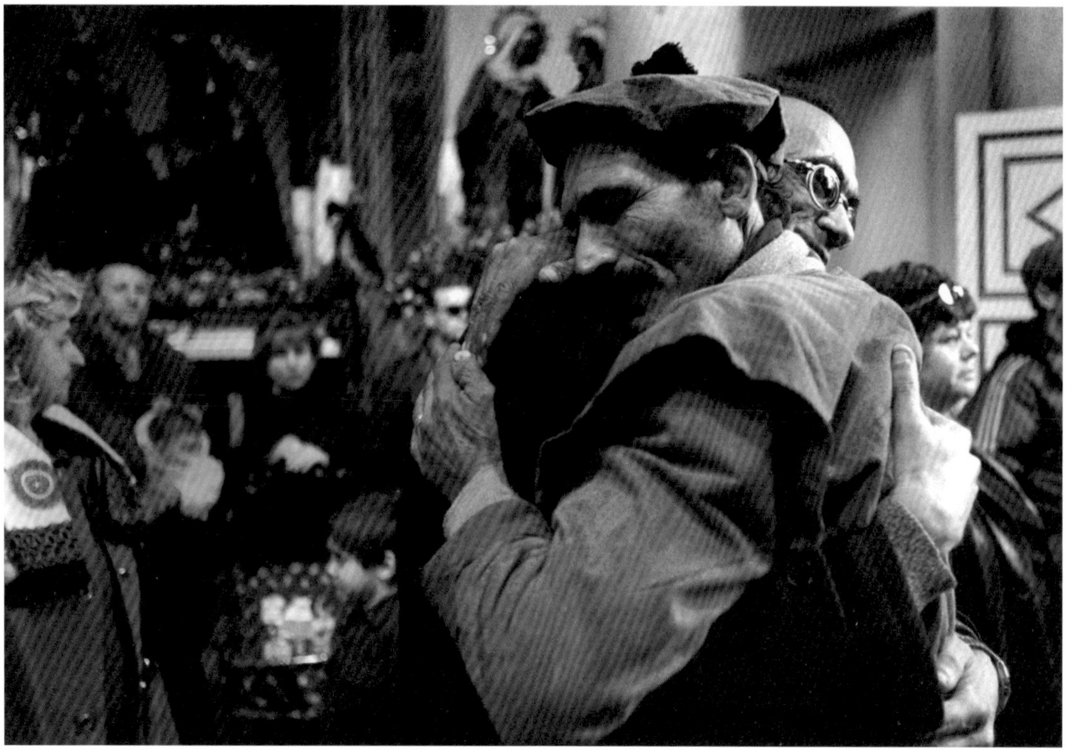

Abbraccio
Trapani

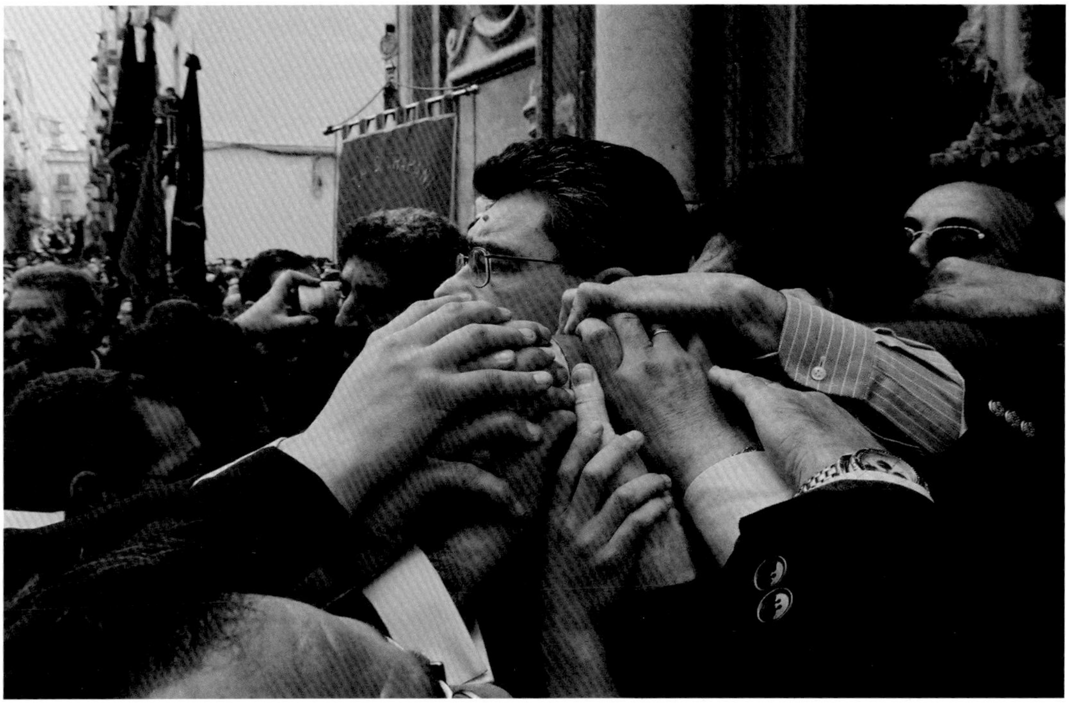

Hands
Trapani

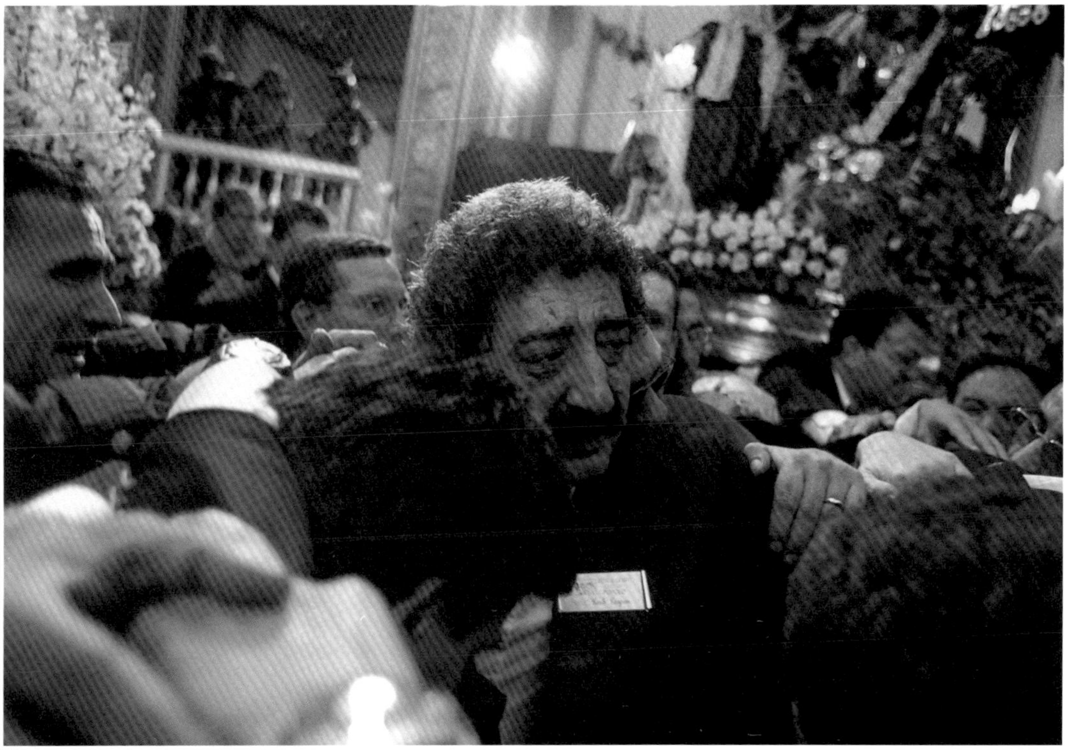

Faccia Dolorosa
Trapani

Page 38 Top:

Beginning before dawn, members of the trade guilds or *ceti* carry heavy floats with wooden statues from twelve to twenty-four hours. Big burly men, sometimes buckling from the weight of their float, move through the streets, swaying back and forth while a Sicilian band follows playing a medieval and monotonous dirge, "A Tear on My Mother's Grave". The hypnotic sway represents the pain of the Madonna who has lost her child. The Holy Saturday climax of the Mysteries ends at the Church of the Corrigio The faces of the statues are twisted in agony as are the tear encrusted faces of the penitents.

Page 38 Bottom:

In the church of Corrigio exhausted penitents weep, embrace and stare transfixed into a place beyond themselves.

Page 39 Top:

On Holy Saturday the last cart carrying the Madonna reaches the Church of Corrigio, she hesitates, rolling back and forth moving with the cadence of the everpresent dirge. Once she enters the church she cannot return to the streets. She isn't sure if her son is in there. Foisted on the shoulders of the ceti or trade guilds she rolls back and forth as if rocking her lost child. The lugubrious sway is hypnotic. The crowds are morose, the atmosphere is melancholy. After hesitating for a half hour or more moves up the stairs and into Corrigio.

Page 39 Bottom:

Inside the church the faces of the bearers are red and swollen. Tears fall onto coats smattered with wax drippings.

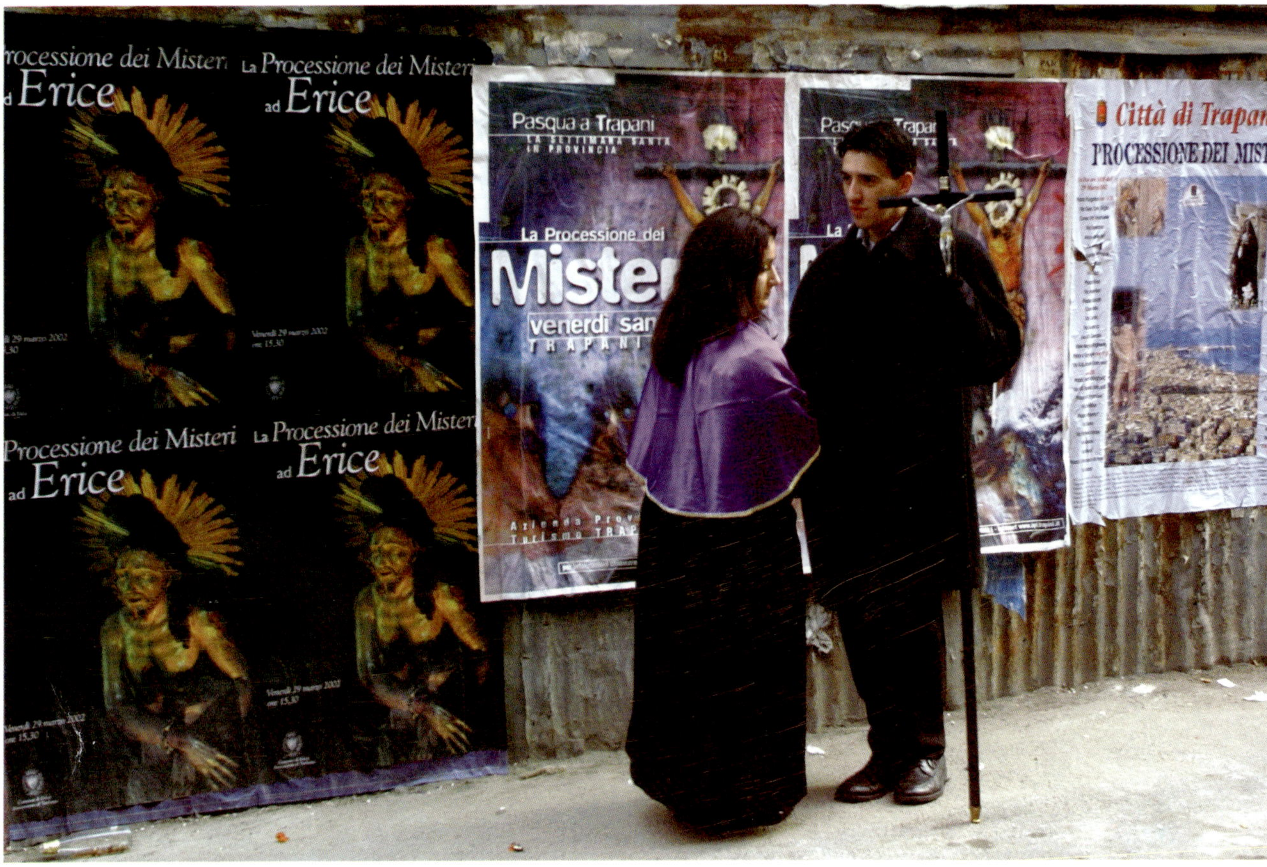

Encounter
Trapani

After a day long reenactment of the life and death of Christ spectators and participants are left sad and bereft. The realism of the agony suffered by Christ leaves onlookers profoundly and emotionally wretched.

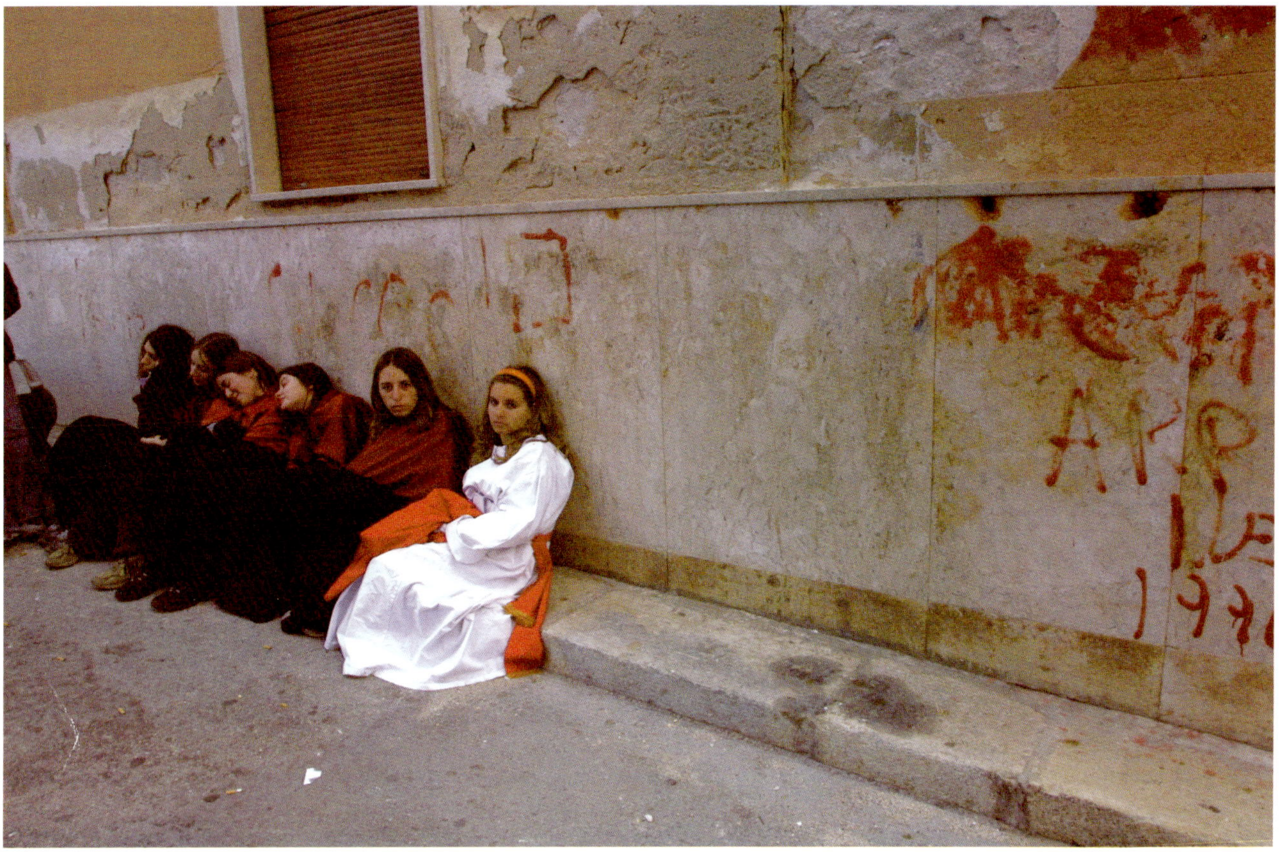

The Writing of the Wall
Marsala

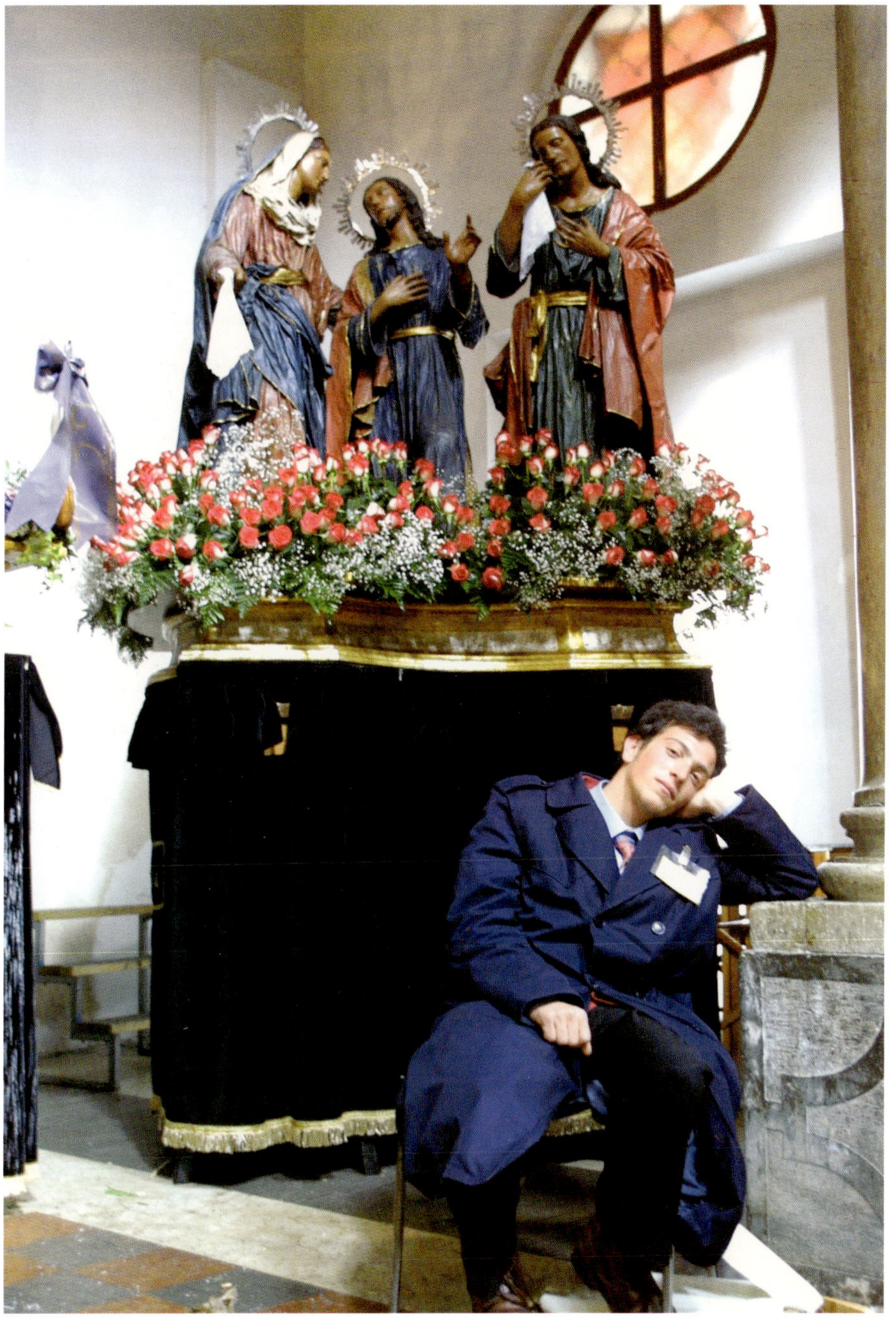

La Festa è Finita
Trapani

Erice, considered one of Italy's most beautiful Medieval hilltowns has been a holyplace from the beginning of time. According to Cadogan, Erice's mythical history dates back to the birth of Venus the beequeen goddess surnamed Eriycina.

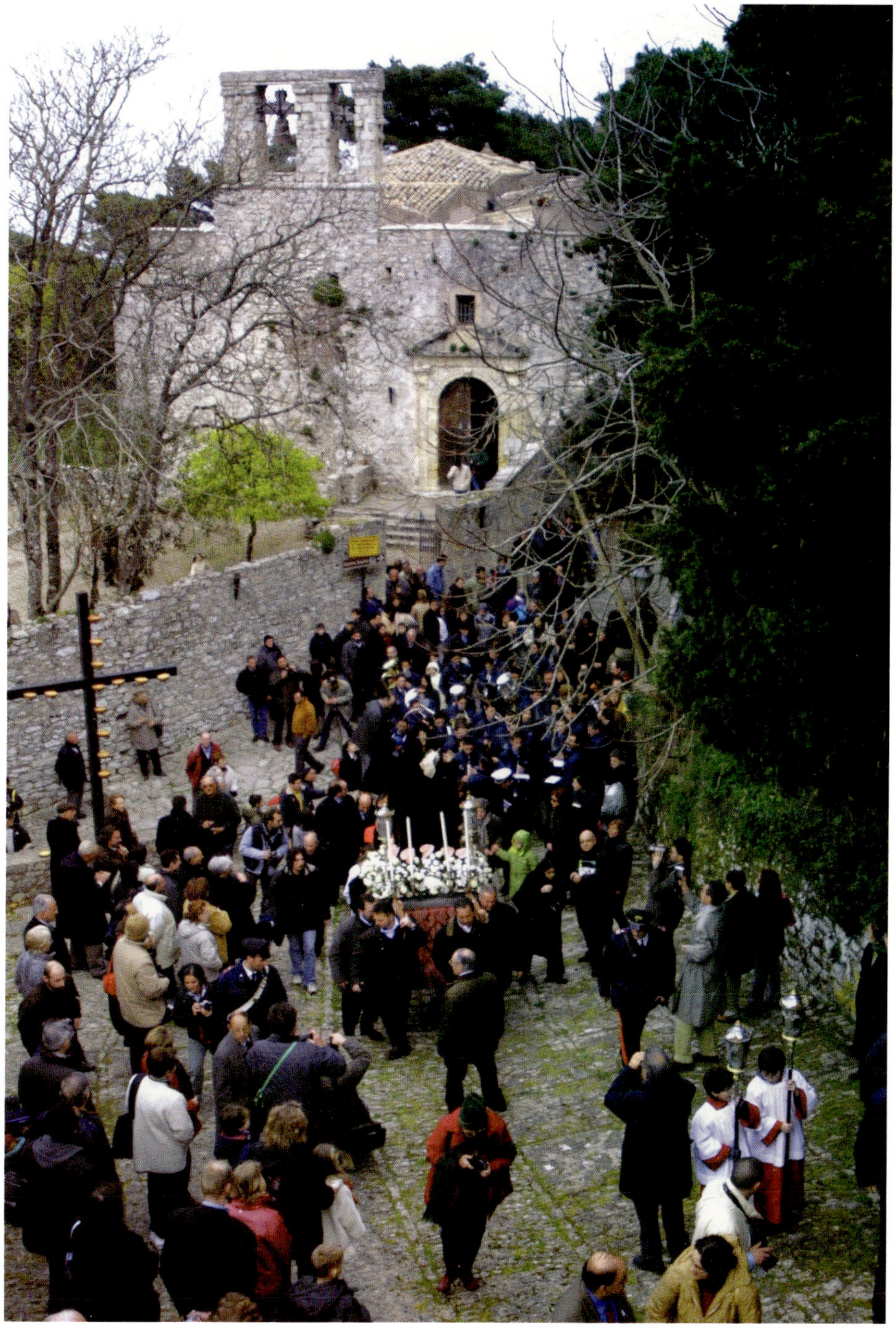

Madonna del Popolo
Erice

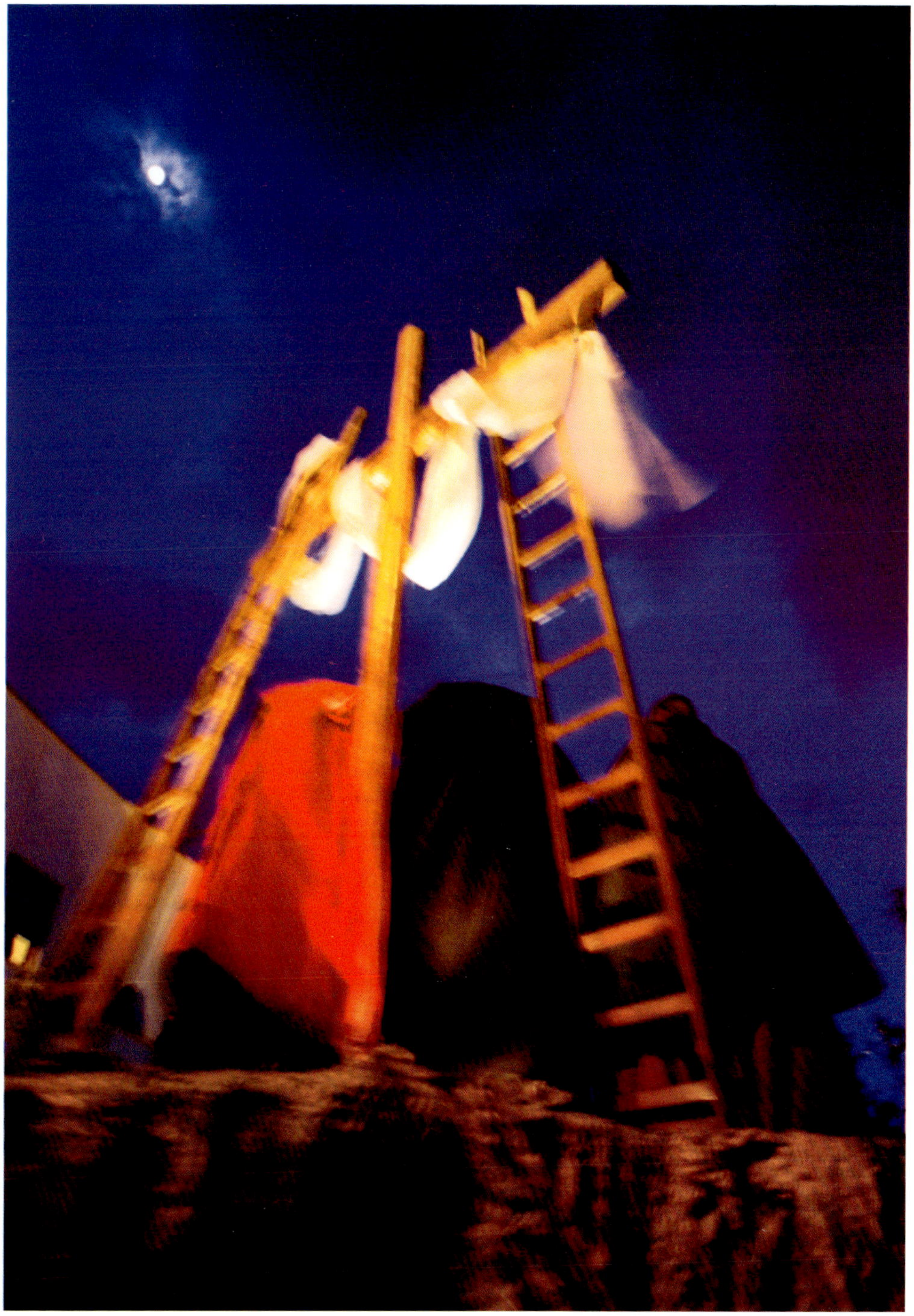

Gesù Deposto Dalla Croce
Busteo Palizollo

Afterward

"First, I think I should tell you how my mother and father happened to come to this country... A family, you understand, is not unlike a plant it has its branches as well as blossoms; it has, above all, its roots."

Joe Pagano in The Golden Wedding

Forever on a personal quest, I am continually exploring the shrouded overgrown labyrinth of matriculation that shaped the values, customs and beliefs of the ones that came before me and sculpted the lives of my grandparents, my parents and ultimately myself.

I ask myself again, as I have so many times in the past, "What is it about this faith, this religion, this church, that has held generations of us in blind deadlock?" Should the Catholic church, bulwark of many of my ancestoral theological doctrines and traditions, be the undisputed definer of God's wishes?

In some way it is as if someone, long before our own birth, had given over that part of our souls and minds. But to whom or what? To God? To the Church? Or perhaps to our own devouring need to comprehend the mystical, timeless cycle of life and death.

Are the myths and the symbolism just smoke and mirrors, adopted by the church to perpetuate her power as "keeper of the myths" or are they anchored in a deep truth that elludes us in its intensity and are, as Joseph Campbell suggests "Masks of God"?

Ripe in legend and myth, Italy's customs and traditions are encapsulated in a patina of Catholicism and Christian folklore commingled with pagan superstition. Naples, Sardinia, Calabria and Sicily are areas where folkloric rituals and beliefs are most galvanized in the ethos of its people. Sicily and Calabria's consist of the southern part of Italy known as the Mezzogiorno. In the Mezzogiorno, the past lingers in the rituals and festivals.

In Calabria, home of my grandparents, penitents flogged themselves until they drew blood. I learned about the "black hand" and the "evil eye" at my Mother's knee. I learned how to use my fingers to form the symbol of the *malocchio* to ward off the evils. In Sicily during Easter Week or the *Feste de Pasqua* (Easter festival) depicts the solemn processions "Christ's Passion" known as the *Mistiri.*

The Story, the real story, is a phenomenon of humanity. Perhaps it is a phenomenon born of a momentary illumination. Participants and spectators are transported to a place beyond themselves—an ethereal, erotic state engendered by emotion, expectation, expiation and exultation. In a sense this work is part of my autobiography; through it meanders the cobblestone path of a journey into self.

Kathleen Amantea Douglas

About the Photographer

I think of myself as a visual historian. My interest in Photography and ultimately my undergraduate degree in Community Planning and graduate degree in Photojournalism came from a curiosity about people and the influences that shaped their lives. As with most of us, that journey started with myself.

In 1993 I traveled with my mother to her parents birthplace in Gioiosa, Italy. I was startled when the ancient town, draped down a mountainous hillside, jogged stories and vignettes from my mother's memory. But even more surprising were my feelings of loss. In Italy, I too, revisited my own youth. In my childhood, I lived in the world my grandparents brought with them to America. When did the wonderful aromas fade away? Where were the old people that sat for hours under the grape arbors exchanging gossip in a lyrical and animated language? Where was Uncle Nick's accordion and the zeippoli. What happened to the home made wine in the green coke bottles with a rag cork? Sadly, I realized that my own son would never know the rich culture that had been his mother's. Never was I more keenly aware of the need to preserve memories and document our lives than at that moment.

The influences of our lives can be seen in the environments we live in, in the environments that shaped our ancestors, in our traditions and rituals and in the expressions of joy, love, surprise, disappointment and yes, anger and sorrow. It is that understanding and a passion to preserve what time cannot that shapes my work. As a portraitist I endeavor to craft a portrait that is about the person, not just his or her image. In some instances taking a portrait a step further into the realm of imagination.

Special events, be they weddings and bar/bat mitzvahs, a company event, a fundraiser, a birthday, a christening, a celebration or a memorial, are as much about the emotion, the elation, the angst as about the event itself. As a journalist, I prefer to let the story unfold. My mission is to look for defining moments and go for the magic.

No fascination with life and beauty could exclude the human body or the creation of new life. Nor has my work. My documentary, portraiture and fine art work is a celebration of life, love and renewal.

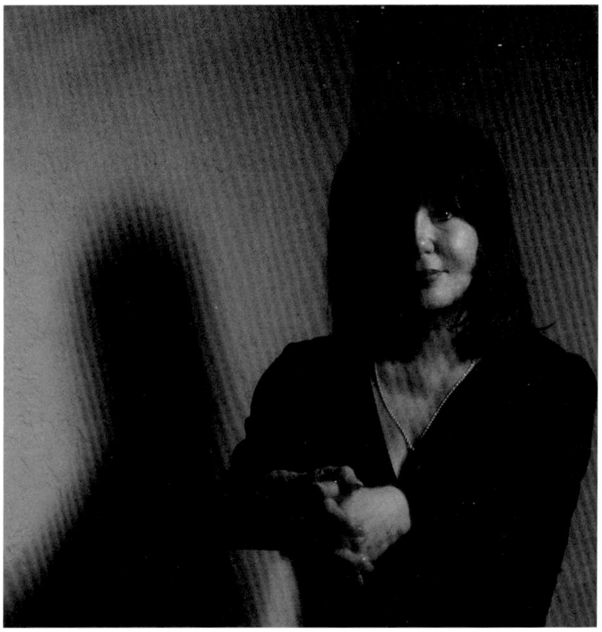

Arthur L. Raineville

Kathleen A. Douglas is a freelance photojournalist, portraitist and fine art photographer. An adventurer and traveler, her work reflects an insatiable curiosity and passion to understand people and their lives. As part of her ethnostudy she has documented life in Haiti, Cuba, the Yucatan, Australia, Hong Kong, Thailand, Vietnam, Africa and Italy. She earned her Master's in Photojournalism at Boston University and continued her studies in Master classes in Boston, Maine and Italy. As a freelancer for Associated Press her work has been published in the Boston Globe, the Patriot Ledger, The Attleboro Sun and other member newspapers. She assists and is a frequent speaker at the New England School of Photography. Her work is on permanent exhibit at the University of Massachusetts and the BU city room In 2003 she will be collaborating on two books documenting, a medical mission in Vietnam and a story of poverty and change in Boston. She works out of her studio in Boston's North End.

For my Mother
Grace M. "Dolly" Amonte
February 14, 1922 - December 23, 2002